RUMI'S BEASTS IN THE MATHNAWI

TRANSLATION AND COMMENTARY BY
I.A. GRAEF

Epigraph Books
Rhinebeck, New York

Paperback ISBN 978-1-960090-78-2

Contact the publisher for Library of Congress Control Number

Epigraph Books
22 East Market Street, Suite 304
Rhinebeck, New York 12572
(845) 876-4861
epigraphpublishing.com

CONTENTS

Introduction   vii

Acknowledgments   xiv

References   xv

BOOK I

The Parrot   2

The Lion and the Beasts   6

The Wolf and the Fox Go Hunting with the Lion   9

BOOK II

The Sufi's Beast   14

The Falcon   18

The Snake   20

The Bear   22

The Lost Camel   24

The Camel and the Mouse   25

The Miracles of Ibrahim   26

The Ducks   28

BOOK III

The Elephant   32
The Jackal Who Pretended to be a Peacock   34
The Snake Catcher   36
The Shape of the Elephant   37
The Mule's Complaint to the Camel   38
The Hare's Ambassador to the Elephants   40
The Dog's Vow   41
The Eagle and the Prophet   41
The Language of the Beasts and Birds   42
 The Gnat and the Wind Before King Solomon   46

BOOK IV

Majnun and his She-Camel   50
The Three Fish   51
The Liberated Bird   53

BOOK V

The Parable of the Four Birds   56
The Arab Who Wept for his Dog   58
The Peacock Who Tore Out Its Feathers   59
The Peacock's Reply   60
The Gazelle in the Donkey Stable   61
The Maid and the Ass   62
The Puppies Who Barked Before They Were Born   66
The Fox and the Ass   67
The Hungry Ass and the Arab Horses   68
The Fox and the Ass   69
The Man Afraid of Being Taken for an Ass   70
 The Cow Alone on the Island of Clover   73
 The Cat and the Meat   74

BOOK VI

The Fowler and the Bird   78

The Man Whose Ram Was Stolen   79

The Camel, the Ox, and the Ram   81

The Mouse and the Frog   82

The Sea Cow   85

The King and the Beautiful Horse   86

The Child and the Bogle   89

INTRODUCTION

Jalalu'ddin Rumi (30 September 1207 – 17 December 1273) was a Persian Muslim poet and a Sufi mystic. He lived most of his life under the Sultanate of Rum, where he produced his works[1] and died in 1273 AD. He was buried in Konya and his shrine has become a place of pilgrimage. Following his death, his followers and his son Sultan Walad founded the Mevlevi Order, also known as the Order of the Whirling Dervishes, famous for the Sema ceremony, a scared cosmic dance.

Although his works are written in Persian, Rumi's importance is considered to transcend national and ethnic borders. His original works are widely read in their original language across the Persian-speaking world. Translations of his works are very popular in other countries. His poems have been widely translated into many of the world's languages and transposed into various formats. In 2007, he was described as the "most popular poet in America."

Jalaluddin Rumi's classic masterpiece poem, *The Mathnawi*, was written in 25,700 verses which are comprised of 6 books in 3 volumes. This treasure chest of stories, parables and anecdotes uses the classic forms of rhetoric established by the ancient Greeks and Romans, namely analogy, cause & effect, example, repetition and humor. This Sufi classic poem is longer than the Illiad and Odyssey combined.

My intention is to provide easier access for the modern reader to this masterpiece written some 800 years ago by updating some language of the original, authoritative Nicholson translation and by focusing on the more simple stories, or animal fables. Thus, this much abridged edition focuses exclusively on the animal stories in the *Mathnawi*, with some added commentary. The approximately forty animal stories don't stand alone, but are used, as with many of the other stories, as examples for some of the deeper themes Rumi addresses.

Frequently stories, thematically related, are woven within stories within stories, so that several stories may be told before the first one ends. Rumi understands that the best ways of learning are by analogy and example. If we know very little about a subject, we can learn more about it by comparing it to something we do know. Often the hardest truth to grasp is a paradoxical one. For example, yes, we are all one, yet each one of us is a unique individual. Other paradoxes to consider: although many people may pray, are the prayers of a hypocrite equal to, or as acceptable as, those of a true believer? Is praying, for example like the Lord's prayer, simply a matter of repeating the words, or should the meaning of the words resonate in the heart?

What does it mean to be a human being? To understand humans, we have to look at animals since all humans are animals, or have an animal nature. Rumi claims we started out as minerals, evolved into plants, and then took animal forms before we became humans. Rumi is concerned with the spiritual evolution of a human being: Man not conscious of God is akin to an animal and true consciousness makes him divine.

According to the Sufis, like Rumi, humans have an animal side and an angelic side. We can be like angels or we can be like beasts, but we cannot be both simultaneously, even though we have both sides within us. That is the paradox: either we are inclined towards the sensual or towards the spiritual. Rumi declares we must sacrifice our sensual side in order to make progress in the spiritual; we cannot be filled with both simultaneously. For example, we cannot glean spiritual truths if we are filled with lustful desires.

In Book IV Rumi quotes the following Hadith of Mustafa (Muhammed) on whom be peace:

Verily, the most high God created the angels and set reason in them, and He created the beasts and set lust in them, and He created the sons of Adam and set in them reason and lust; and he whose reason prevails over his lust is higher than the angels, and he whose lust prevails over his reason is lower than the beasts.

In the twenty-first century, where science and technology has become the new religion, we tend to lose sight of, or forget, our inherent animal nature. Before the advent of the industrial revolution we walked or rode horses, while today we zip around in our automobiles. We easily lose touch with our animal nature if we don't actively physically exercise, for our bodies are the animals we ride. Many people get stuck in their heads by limiting themselves to their computer/television/smart phones and cars. Rather than making us smarter, all these machines make us more mechanical and more dependent on, or enslaved, to said machines. We may feel connected to a larger cyber community, yet that's an artificial, not a human, connection, no matter how enhanced or real it feels; hence the internet can increase our alienation and isolation. We cannot develop harmoniously if our mental, emotional and physical bodies are not balanced.

Today science claims that some substantial, though tangential, proof of the great Mysteries, finally can be provided, albeit on a purely sensory level. Proof is essential to modern science, yet how many of these scientists actually have a conscious, beating heart anymore. For example, do they feel for, or have empathy for, the monkeys or other animals in their labs?

As we lose touch with our true nature, we don't hesitate to pollute and spoil our beautiful planet, knocking her out of balance, out of her natural rhythm. In this world out of balance it's no wonder that thousands of animal species become extinct every year. Ironically, as scientists are discovering, often after the fact, many of these plant and animal species have a lot to teach us. Indigenous cultures knew this intuitively. Native Americans honor the earth as their mother. Many readers may groan and say, yes, we know all that. But if we knew all that, why do we continue to destroy our environment ? Why did we, and do we, continue to think that we are superior just because of our technology ? Unlike us, those 'primitive' cultures did not forget about their true animal nature. They know animals have a lot to teach us.

Animals are in touch with their essential nature and act instinctively, intuitively, out of necessity to survive. Most people, on the other hand, think way too much. Thus, it's not surprising that modern humans who over think, or get stuck in their heads, typically have some self-defeating personality disorder, usually, but not always in a mild, fairly harmless form, whether it's obsessive compulsion, narcissism, or paranoid schizophrenia, etc. Most people suffer from some sort of delusion, making them unable to perceive reality correctly, much less their place in nature. If they're not the captain of their own vessel, how can they reach safe harbor?

Forgetting our animal nature does not make it disappear. On the contrary, denying and suppressing it makes it leap forth, or erupt, in odd perverse ways, as evidenced by the strange effects of the strong inhibitions of the Victorians, i.e. in Stevenson's *Dr. Jekyl and Mr. Hyde*. We must accept our animal side, yet make sure it has its proper place; that is, we must master our sensual side, or by analogy, ride the horse.

Gurdjieff relies on the analogy of the horse, cart and driver to explain our situation. "Inside us we have a horse; it obeys orders from outside." The horse needs to be educated, but the driver has forgotten how to teach it more than how to go left or right. "Inner change refers only to the need of change in the horse. If the horse changes, we can change even externally...The horse must change." The driver is the mind, the intellect, which can be filled with knowledge, and still be useless, because he, "even if he knows, cannot drag the cart without the horse – it's too heavy".

First of all you must realize that you are not you. Be sure of that,
believe me. You are the horse, and if you wish to start working,
the horse must be taught a language in which you can talk to it,
tell it what you know and prove to it the necessity of changing
its disposition.

(Gurdjieff, In Search of the Miraculous 96-97)

The cart, representing the physical body, is also an important part of the team and needs to be educated. Only the driver can do this, but not alone. Most of the time the driver is lazy and asleep. He must always remember his destination, and usually needs someone else to remind him. The horse is our essential, emotional nature without which the journey is impossible.

Our animal nature is as fascinating and intriguing as our spiritual nature. Anthropomorphic stories have been a staple of almost every culture. Magical transformations are a common feature of ancient Egyptian storytelling, where humans are changed into animals or vice versa. Homer had Circe transform Ulysses' men into swine, and Apuleius had his hero transformed into a golden ass in his bawdy first century novel by the same name. We must come to accept and embrace our animal nature.

Clever talking animals, like Coyote, play significant roles in many Native American tales. The Hindus revered some animals in their stories as gods, i.e. Hanuman (monkey god) and Ganesh (elephant like god). Perhaps a quarter of Rumi's *Mathnawi* has stories dealing with animals. In truth, though, most of Rumi's stories were 'borrowed', or not his own. Many Sufi stories and fables, like Aesop's (a thousand years prior to Rumi), came from a rich oral tradition, very much alive in the Middle East when Rumi completed his *Mathnawi* (1273 A.D.) *The Thousand and One Nights*, another classic example of an anthology of fantastic tales, has many magical animals. Very rarely were the authors of these stories given credit. Similarly, *Aesop's Fables* are an anthology of animal stories handed down from ancient times.

While such fables can amuse and entertain children, they also provide keen insights into the human psyche.

The German writer, Schiller, noted extravagantly that, "Deeper meaning lies in the fairy tales of my childhood than in the truth that is taught in life" (*The Piccolomini*, III,40). Most likely, he was referring to *Grimm's Fairy Tales*, yet another famous anthology full of clever talking animals. Like parables, myths and fairy tales can be understood on more than one level. A child can simply be entertained by a fairy tale, while on a deeper psychological level realize certain human truths which an adult could otherwise never explain. Rumi states: *"Children stories contain many mysteries and moral lessons. Although they say many ridiculous things, treasures are to be sought in such ruined places." (III:2602)*

Similarly Jesus spoke in parables for he realized people were not ready to accept simple truths such as, "love your neighbor". Symbolic language was necessary to convey higher truths. So Rumi drew from this vast pool of rich, symbolic literature to allude to religious teachings (usually Islamic), all designed to cultivate our higher nature. At the time he was writing, the Crusades combined with mercantile trade routes enabled Eastern and Western cultures to share a great deal of literature.

The Mathnawi is filled with many more treasures than simple animal tales, and all sorts of characters populate the stories. My focus is predominantly on the beasts since that is a good starting point. Acknowledging our own animal nature is a good beginning to recovering our humanity. In this mechanical world with its emphasis on technology, it's more important than ever *not* to lose touch with our humanity, *not* to forget our heart.

By populating our world more with machines at the expense of animals, people have become more like machines, having lost touch with their animal nature. Although most of the world is steeped in sleep and follow like cattle their own lustful desires, ironically they have forgotten their own animal nature. By first remembering we are animals, we can then recall what makes us higher than animals, and it's not just our ability to reason. Higher emotions combined with thought is the divine elixir. Clearly, people must awaken to their own divine nature before they are able to perceive the deeper secrets and treasures of the *Mathnawi*. In fact, the thesis of the *Mathnawi* urges us to accept and cultivate our divine nature.

In order to come in touch with our divine nature, however, Rumi and other Sufis suggest, first we must slay, or subjugate, our animal desires or ego. As a pious, ascetic preacher, Rumi was merciless with his body, routinely denying it food and sleep. The body must learn who's the boss, which is why we must practice strict self-control. We must repent of our sins and find righteous, awakened companions to remind us of our goal: to become conscious of our divinity. Most religions have their share of ascetic recluses who remove themselves from the world to progress on the spiritual path, but Islam has no monks or monasteries. Thus, Sufis are encouraged 'to be in the world, but not of the world'.

Clearly sainthood is not for everyone, and we need not become deeply religious to enjoy Rumi's fantastic tales. The master offers us many deep lessons about our humanity and place in the world. We should accept his observations with humility and respect, recognizing that despite all our technology, the progress of our evolution has been fairly insignificant in the last 800 years.

ACKNOWLEDGMENTS

What authority do I have to translate, or interpret, the work of the great Master and Sheikh, Jellaludin Rumi?

I entered the Sufi Path when I reached the age of responsibility, or adulthood, 50 years ago. Since then I was initiated into several, different *Tariqat*s, or Sufi Orders. At that time, my earliest, beloved, spiritual mentor, who wasn't a Sufi, cautioned me, that you can only really initiate yourself when you're ready. No one can do it for you, as no one can walk the spiritual path, or do the Work, for you.

In 1974 Pir Vilayat Inayat Khan, head of the Sufi Order of the West, initiated me and gave me a *wazifa*, like a *mantra*, to repeat daily a certain number of times. Through the Pir I found my Palestinian Sheikh Hasan, whom I later visited at his refugee camp in Nablus on the West Bank. Sheikh Hasan claimed to be a *Murshid*, or master in seven different Sufi Orders. With his *Bayat*, or initiation, I was also drawn into those *Tariqats*. During the 1970's I also became involved with a Turkish *Tariqat, the Helveti Jerrahi*, into which I was later initiated. In the 1980's I was inducted into the *Naqshabandi Order* of Grand Sheikh Nazim of Dagestan. Having had the blessings of these great Sufi sheikhs, as well as other lesser known spiritual masters, makes me confident in my ability to provide a brief introduction and analysis of some of Rumi's stories. Additionally, I have loved and studied Rumi all those years.

REFERENCES

Aesop's Fables

The Arabian Nights Entertainment, translated by Lane, Edward William, Jefferson Press, NY

Grimm's Fairy Tales, Random House, NY, 1972.

The Holy Bible. King James Version, Thomas Nelson Inc., USA. 1994

The Holy Quran, translated by Yusuf Ali, Abdullah, McGregor& Werner, Inc., USA 1946

The Mathnawi of Jalaluddin Rumi, translated by Nicholson, Reynolds, A.E.J.W. Gibb Memorial Trust, Great Britain, 1926.

Ouspensky, P.D., *In Search of the Miraculous*, Harcourt, Brace & World, New York, 1949

Schiller, Friedrich, *The Piccolomini*, translated by S.T. Coleridge Paternoster, London 1800

BOOK I

THE PARROT

Ironically, a parrot is the first major animal character in the first couple of stories of Book 1. That Rumi chose a parrot to start this major work is ironic since parrots are famous for repeating everything. They learn by repetition and imitation, yet like many animals they also have feelings. Rumi states the parrot is a metaphor for the soul; like the body, the soul follows the spirit (the supreme intellect), but it gives feedback and tells us when something's wrong. Then we feel pain and suffer.

Since most of the stories in the *Mathnawi* were 'borrowed', the book can be considered an anthology and Rumi a parrot for copying these tales. That, however, is a short sighted view for the stories are simply a starting point for the Master to expound upon many complex themes and ideas. Remember the entire six books (over 1500 pages) are in verse and rhyme in the original. If indeed that's why he started his masterpiece with parrot stories, he was being extremely humble and didn't want to take himself too seriously.

Humor is an integral part of the Mathnawi and also necessary for learning. Rumi's exquisite sense of humor makes the stories come alive, while at the same time explaining profound paradoxes. Humor is usually a result of a paradoxical yes/no situation. We learn by imitating, but only up to a point. If we imitate everything mindlessly, life becomes absurd. This absurdity is illustrated in the story, "The Green Grocer and his Parrot":

The grocer had a sweet, smooth talking parrot perched on a bench in his shop who addressed his customers with wit and charm. One day while the grocer stepped out, the cat in the shop jumped too close to the parrot. Upset the parrot flew to a higher perch and in doing so spilled some bottles of rose oil on the bench. When the master returned and seated himself, he noticed the oil on the bench and that it had stained his clothes. Angrily he went after the parrot and gave the bird such a blow on the head that all the feathers on its head fell off. The bald parrot was so stunned, it spoke no more. For a week or two the grocer sighed and repented of his angry action. A few days later a bald headed holy man passed through the shop. The parrot suddenly screeched, "Hey fellow, whose oil jar did you upset ?" All the bystanders laughed at the parrot's mistake in confusing its own baldness caused by injury with that of the man's caused naturally by age.

Yes, we can learn through observation and imitation, but we have to make clear distinctions and avoid jumping to conclusions. In Disney's *Fantasia* the magician's apprentice tries to imitate his master's magic with disastrous results. After his parrot story Rumi continues to caution against making false analogies. For example, although all saints are human, we cannot conclude all humans are saints, since only very few rise to that station.

In this world the bitter sea and the sweet sea are divided – between them is a barrier which they do not seek to cross. (297)

This is yet another analogy to the divide between the sensual world and the spiritual world. So, too, good men deserve good women, while wicked men go with wicked women. People wear masks to hide their identities, so it's often hard to distinguish between them, and we should not rush to judgment. Similarly, in the woods for every good, edible mushroom is one that looks like it, but is poisonous. So, too, in the world are honest, holy men as well as evil charlatans, or wicked priests.

The work of holy men is light and heat; the work of vile men is trickery and shameless [scams]. (320)

Attempting to distinguish truth from falsehood can often lead to bewilderment. Everyone wants to be on the path of certainty. However, since we do not have the eye of certainty, we slavishly imitate others. We parrot back what we've learned from our parents or teachers. Our society conditions us to follow blindly and not to question authority. Mental slavery is imposed upon us in many ways. For example, our computers and phone gadgets are supposed to make life easier and us more connected, yet paradoxically these machines can complicate our lives and can make us feel more alienated and alone than ever. Ironically, we become prisoners in cages of our own making. The second parrot story points the way to our liberation.

A merchant loved the pretty parrot caged in his shop. When the merchant prepared to travel to India, he asked the parrot what present he should bring back for her. The parrot had only one request: "When you see the parrots there, explain my plight, that I'm in prison here, longing for them." When the merchant reached India and saw the parrots on a plain, he delivered this message. On hearing it, one of them immediately fell down dead. The merchant was irritated and distraught he'd inadvertently caused this parrot's death. Upon returning home, he rebuked his own parrot for having sent this fatal message. When his parrot heard of the other parrot's demise, she too fell down dead in her cage. Weeping in sorrow, the merchant took the parrot outside to bury her. To his surprise, the parrot quickly recovered and flew away into a tree. The parrot told him: "My sister in India counseled me – 'abandon your charming voice and affection for

your master, for this is the cause of your bondage'. She feigned her
death to suggest the path to my own liberation."

"Die before you die", is the message of mystics of the ages. In
other words, we must die to our lower carnal self, so we can liberate
ourselves from the world's bondage. Care not for world's honor or
reputation, for that's all vanity. All is vanity, is said in the Bible, and in
truth that's how much of this foolish world runs, after this and that,
losing sight of the Beloved. Rumi's second parrot story (above) runs
for more than ten pages in the original, because he weaves in many
spiritual truths and pearls of wisdom. His words are a guide for liberation: we must not yield to all these earthy temptations of the lower
self if we are to make progress in the spiritual realm. "Self-control
is the thing desired by the intelligent...whoever practices self-control ascends to heaven..." (1601) Children love candy, yet it's really
unhealthy. Sure, we can be greedy, gluttonous, arrogant and selfish,
but such vices only hasten our destruction. Do we have a choice in
such matters? We must do what "it" (ego) does not like and oppose
what "it" wants. Only if we have developed a will can we choose and
we can develop a will only through discipline and by denying the
wishes of our lower self. All vanity is destruction of the soul.

Rumi says, the parrot, whose voice comes from Divine inspiration, is hidden within us. We are captive to whomever we love; our
beloved has a powerful influence upon us. We wish to get caught in
torrents of divine ecstasy of union with our beloved, yet we practice
self-control so we do not drown therein. Paradoxically, this sweet
death is what we need most since only divine love can break the
chains of mental slavery, i.e. fixation on material things, like money,
can shatter our delusions.

The whole world became jealous because God is superior to all
the world in jealousy. He is like the spirit, and the world is like the
body: the body receives from the spirit both good and evil. (1764)

In other words, since man was made in God's image, man also has some jealousy. Thus, we are tormented by our beloved's absence and easily entertain fantasies of petty jealousy. However, we must transcend sorrow and joy, for "love is higher than these two states of feeling". (1794) Sorrow and joy come and go, but "there is another state of consciousness which is rare". (1804) This can be attained when we are in a state of constant remembrance and do not identify with these passing emotions, which are like shadows on a wall. We must strive to remember every single breath.

This seems a difficult if not impossible trick, since we are so easily swayed by our beloved's and other people's affections and praise. Once again self-control is necessary, yet in a moment "the world's flattery and hypocrisy is a sweet morsel", and we become full of arrogance. The Devil (ego) has myriad ways to hasten our self-destruction. Thus, we must become immune to praise or blame.

This idea is wonderfully illustrated in the following fable.

THE LION AND THE BEASTS

In a valley a lion continually harassed and mercilessly hunted the beasts until one day they made a compact and said to the lion: "If you stop hunting us, we will keep you well fed with a daily allowance. We will sacrifice one of us to you daily, if you leave us alone." The lion was suspicious and replied: "I am done to death by the cunning and fraud of men; I am bitten by the sting of (human) snake and scorpion. But worse than all men in fraud and spite is the man of the flesh (nafs) lying in wait for me." The beasts answered that he should relax and trust in God, or Divine Providence. Yes, added the lion, trusting in God is fine, but that does not mean to become lazy and indolent.

Rumi considers at some length this age old argument between the lion and the beasts, whether it's better to rely on one's own efforts rather than divine destiny, or trust in God. Over many centuries philosophers have never completely resolved this argument of free will vs. destiny. Gurdjieff, for instance, like the lion insisted that man has no choice or free will, and that man can only succeed by making efforts. Rumi presents both sides of the argument with excellent examples and prophetic allusions.

> *The beasts, however, won their argument and finally persuaded him to trust in God rather than his own efforts, since they convinced the lion he could always return to hunting if he didn't get his daily allowance. So, one by one, they sacrificed themselves to the lion until one day it was the hare's turn to die. The hare, however, protested: "How long must we endure this injustice?"*
>
> *The company of beasts urged him not to delay his sacrifice, not to anger the lion. The hare, however, had a plan. "O friends", said he, "grant me a respite, that by my cunning you may escape from calamity." The beasts scoffed that the hare was becoming conceited and again urged him not to delay his obligations. The hare argued eloquently in his defense until the beasts consented to let him try his luck.*
>
> *Because they'd argued so long, the hare was late, and the lion was roaring with rage. The hare apologized, saying his brother hare who had accompanied him had been attacked and dragged off by another lion. The lion furiously commanded the hare to show him this other lion so he could punish this transgressor of his domain. The hare, pretending great fear, jumped on the lion's back and directed him to a deep well.*

"Knowledge is the seal of the kingdom of Solomon: the whole world is form, and knowledge is the spirit." (*1030*) Only by subjugating our sensuality, driving our bodies rather than the other way around, can we receive wisdom or spiritual guidance. The commanding self must operate with absolute certainty.

Here Rumi diverges from this tale to tell another, the story of King Solomon and the hoopoe bird, which is related to this theme of the certainty of divine destiny. When all the birds were relating one by one in secret to King Solomon their various talents, the hoopoe claimed that by destiny he had the eye of certainty, which could see into great depths and distances. Thus, the hoopoe was most highly prized among birds by Solomon. The beauty of the *Mathnawi* is Rumi's ability to subtly weave in a multitude of strands of stories within stories. Before returning to the story of the lion and hare, the story of how Adam learned the names of everything is related. Destiny has provided the names of things and so the power of them.

> *When they approached the well, the hare drew back and the lion demanded to know why. The hare claimed: "That lion lives in this well: within this fortress he is safe from harm." Everyone who is wise chose to live in the well, because spiritual joys are attained only in solitude. (1299) "Come on," said the lion, "my blow subdues him. Let's look together down this well." In the well the lion saw his own reflection with a plump hare by his side. The moment he glimpsed his fierce rival, the lion jumped at him, or into the well, obviously to his doom. At that moment the lion couldn't distinguish himself from his adversary. His reflection became his adversary. With delight the hare ran to share the good news with the beasts. All the beasts went wild with glee and praised the hare to heaven.*

Rumi expounds upon this idea that the fault we see in others are really our own. It's always easier to spot the faults of others than in ourselves. We're blind to the evil within us, otherwise we would hate ourselves. Faithful friends will help us in this instance. Rumi quotes the hadith: "The faithful are mirrors to one another." (1327)

Another hadith is quoted: "*We have returned from the lesser jihad to the greater jihad.*" The greater jihad is the struggle with beast or enemy within. Remember: man has a bestial side as well as an angelic side. In order to reach his true divine nature, every man must slay the beast (lion), or carnal nature within. Rumi shows us how to escape our mental slavery, how to escape from the narrow cage of worldly reputation. His words guide us to liberation from the wiles of our domineering ego.

The commanding self thus must be in the driver's seat, subjugating its selfish, physical desires for the higher good. The selfish ego must be cut down or slain before it gains influence. This theme of self-sacrifice is wonderfully illustrated in the following fable.

THE WOLF AND THE FOX GO HUNTING WITH THE LION

The lion, wolf and fox went hunting together in the mountains. They caught a mountain ox, a goat and a fat hare. The wolf and fox hoped the lion would divide the spoils with justice, but the lion only smiled. Do not trust the smiles of a lion! Finally the lion asked the wolf to be his deputy and devise a way to divide their bounty. The wolf said the wild ox, the largest animal, should go to the lion, while the goat should be his, the wolf's, and the fox should get the hare. The lion was displeased with the lion's judgment and tore him to pieces. "How can he speak of 'I' and 'you' when I am here?" muttered the lion. "I thought we were all one."

The lesson here is the necessity of dissolving the ego. In the midst of this story Rumi inserts the following noteworthy anecdote with this same theme:

> *A person knocked at a friend's door. The friend asked who was there, and outside the man said, "It is I". "I won't open the door for any 'I'", was the reply. The man went away for a year and returned to knock at the door. "Who's there?" came from within. "You are at the door, O beloved," he answered, and the door opened. Moral: there is no room for "you" and "I" when we are one.*
>
> *Return to the story of the lion who tore of the wolf's head for his disrespect. Then he turned to the fox and asked him to divide their prey. The fox wisely offered all to the King of Beasts for breakfast, lunch and dinner. The lion was pleased and asked from whom he'd learned to divide spoils so justly. "O king of the world", he replied, "I learned it from the wolf." The lion was so pleased he gave all three carcasses to the fox. "How can I hurt you fox since you have become mine?" The fox gave thanks to himself that his judgment had been called upon after the wolf's.*

In most fables or fairy tales the lion always has the title of King of the Beasts, but the fox is usually more clever and can outwit him. In the story above this fox's luck depended on his self-restraint. On a deeper level the wolf represents the body with its basic desires, the fox represents the intellect and the lion the emotions. We may spout all sorts of intellectual ideas with ease, but their influence is reduced to zero when we feel pangs of hunger. Our best intentions come to naught when confronted with our body's needs. Gurdjieff tells the following Armenian fairy tale to illustrate this:

> *Once there lived a wolf who slaughtered a great many sheep and reduced many people to tears. For some reason he suddenly*

felt qualms of conscience and began to repent his life; so he decided to reform and slaughter no more sheep. In order to do this seriously he went to a priest and asked him to hold a thank giving service. The priest began the service and the wolf stood weeping and praying in the church. The service was long. The wolf had slaughtered many of the priest's sheep, so the priest prayed earnestly the wolf would indeed reform. Suddenly the wolf looked through the window and saw the sheep were being driven home. He began to fidget, but the priest went on and on without end. At last the wolf could contain himself no longer and shouted: "Finish it, priest! Or all the sheep will be driven home and I shall be left without supper!" (Miraculous 366)

The wolf, like the donkey in Rumi's story, repented of having repented. Both these animals were overwhelmed by their animal desires, as often many people are.

Usually our physical needs take priority, then our emotional needs, and many people remain intellectually deprived and think nothing of it. To rein supreme our higher emotions must work together with the intellect, and bodily needs are negligible. Emotions are a powerful influence, and especially negative emotions can bring us to ruin. Although we are ruled mostly by our emotions, only the intellect can clean up the mess we can get into when we become overly emotional. The fox (intellect) and lion (emotions) have to work together to restrain and sublimate our physical impulses.

BOOK II

THE SUFI'S BEAST

A wandering Sufi thought himself fortunate to find a Khanaqa (Sufi monastery) to spend the night. He tied his ass in the stable and joined his new friends at the dinner table. Before digging into the feast, the Sufi asked one of the servants to see about his beast, to make sure it, too, had food and drink. He gave meticulous instructions on how to treat his old ass. "Of course, of course, it's already taken care of," the servant assured him. "I'm on my way back there now." Of course, the rascal never went to the stable, but instead mocked the Sufi's instructions to his friends. After dinner, weary from his journey, the Sufi stretched out to sleep. He had awful dreams: a wolf was tearing at his ass's ass. He recalled, though, the servant had promised to care for his ass, and why wouldn't he?

Meanwhile the poor, old ass was gasping under the heavy saddle and pack yet to be removed. He groaned with pain and torment for lack of food and water and rolled on his side all night. In the morning the servant gave him a few sharp whacks to get him on his feet. When the Sufi came and mounted his ass and was set to depart, the ass kept falling on his face, and the Sufi couldn't get very far that day.

R umi admonishes us that the world is filled with wicked hypocrites. They pretend to be holy and loving, but are ready to set us up for a fall and laugh at our expense. We should not be so naïve to assume that just because someone claims to be a Sufi, or some sort of holy guru, that he'll guide us to any place but the outhouse. Usually they're only interested in money, since they have no desire to do an honest day's work.

He gives the following anecdote to show how easily our senses can deceive us:

A peasant tied his ox in the stable. A lion came and ate the ox and sat in its place. In the evening the peasant went to the stable to see the ox. He was groping around in the dark, rubbing the fur, but really his hands were all over the lion, who was mildly amused.

Again, Rumi suggests that truth and certainty come from within, and that it's naïve to rely on our senses alone. The truth is within and that's where we must look. The best teachers know that the student knows everything already on a deeper level; the teacher has to open the door to that level.

Another wandering Sufi arrived at the Khanaqa and led his ass to the stable. He, himself, gave it food and water. He was more cautious and less trusting than that other Sufi. These Khanaqa Sufis were poor and destitute. They regularly sold visiting travelers' beasts, and as soon as the Sufi left the stable, sold his little ass. With the proceeds they bought gourmet food and decked their table with finery. Jubilantly they cried: "Tonight we have a grand feast with song and dance! We're weary of fasting. We have a soul and guests to entertain." They were most pleasant and affectionate to their guest who got caught up in their merriment. They all feasted and danced, stamping their feet, tumultuous souls whirling in ecstasy. After they'd been dancing for a long while, the minstrel struck up a deep, sonorous tune. He started to sing: "The ass is gone, the ass is gone." He made the whole company sing along with enthusiasm as they danced: "The ass is gone, the ass is gone, O son!" Imitating their deep feeling, the Sufi guest too began to sing these verses passionately. They sang and danced all night long until the dawn and time to say farewell.

In the morning the monastery was deserted and the Sufi found himself alone with his dusty baggage. He hurried to the stable to catch up with his fellow travelers, but could not find his ass. He thought the servant must've taken him to the watering hole. He found the servant and asked: "Where is my ass ?" The servant shrugged and glanced at him with chagrin.

"Look, I trusted you with my ass. Now where is he?" insisted the Sufi.

"I was overpowered by the Sufis and I was afraid for my life," claimed the servant.

"Am I to suppose the Sufis took my ass from you by violence? Why then didn't you come and tell me this last night? I am discovering this kind of late now that they are gone. Couldn't you have informed me earlier of this terrible outrage?"

"By God, I came more than once to tell you of this deed, but you were always shouting with more gusto than the others: the ass is gone. So I thought you knew of this, that they had told you."

"Everyone said it so merrily, so I simply followed their lead. Blind imitation has brought me to ruin," said the Sufi dejectedly.

We are social animals and, as such, wish to belong to some larger group, where we can work together and have our talents be appreciated. Some can join a gardening club, or others the football team. Most organizations have leaders and a certain hierarchy. Thus, most members and most people are followers. We learn by following guidance from above and by imitating others around us. Certainly, no harm can come from following, unless we do so blindly and naively.

The *Sufi's Beast* is about naïveté on the spiritual path and the rogues who take advantage of innocent seekers. Many people follow different spiritual paths, such as Buddhist, Hindu, Pagan, Sufi, etc., in the course of which they are chanting foreign words they don't understand. Automatically they join in and mumble along since they don't want to be left out. Of course, all these paths, even the Catholic with its Latin Mass, assume a requisite amount of faith from the believers, or followers. They're asked to believe in an abstract God or gods. In the twenty-first century, where science and technology has become the new religion, we're also asked to believe the scientists, even though we can't always understand their methodology behind the reduction of the great mysteries to external measurements.

"The Sufi is the son of the moment", is a famous saying, which means he must be present in every moment in every breath, even if his state becomes ecstatic. Full consciousness must be maintained in states of ecstasy as well as in sorrow and suffering. All this is easier said than done and may take years of practice.

Of course, most of us would prefer a short cut, if possible, and some groups offer that. Frequently, Sufi and other spiritual groups become cults, meaning inordinate pressure is exerted on members to conform and *contribute* [even commit suicide as in Jonestown or Waco]. After all, Sufis and other spiritual groups have to survive, and more than a few are not above a bit of scamming in order to survive. Such scamming Sufis, like those in the story, are probably not conscious of the suffering their selfishness causes.

Or we can interpret the preceding story with the axiom, "nothing is for free". The Sufi had a grand time *and* learned a valuable lesson; hence, he had to pay for this experience. That, however, seems more of a rationalization for the big con. In reality all spiritual, inspirational experiences, like kirtans, zikrs, sweat lodges, come from God and are supposed to be freely given. The leaders of these 'bridges to divinity' may ask for donations to cover expenses, but should not deny admission to anyone for lack of funds.

Obviously, the trickster element, common in most folk traditions, is at play in this Sufi story. Carl Jung considered understanding the trickster archetype essential to psychological development.

In contrast to the naive fool in the folk tales, the trickster is a mischievous shape shifter, "both subhuman and superhuman, a bestial and divine being, whose chief and most alarming characteristic is his unconsciousness". In animal form he's most often represented by the fox, or in Native American tales, the coyote. His successful efforts to fool everyone ironically fail with the innocent fool in the fairy tale. In the preceding story, however, the Sufi is too conventional in his formatory apparatus to qualify as a total idiot, which is why he's easily fooled. In other words, we need to see the 'big picture' beyond our own narrow goals and not be too gullible.

Birds, like the falcon, have a larger view or scope, because they fly high above all. Falcon hunting is an ancient sport among the Arabs. The falcon is released to hunt and later returns with its prey to its master. Unlike falcons, owls are low flying predators who prefer to hunt in the dark of night. Although considered wise in some traditions, in the following falcon story they represent the conventional mores and intelligence of the common man.

THE FALCON

The falcon (seeker of God) always returns to the King: the falcon who becomes lost is blind. The falcon got dust in his eyes and lost in the wild marshes, fell among the owls. The owls, fearful of a transgressor in their territory, attacked him. Though the falcon protested vehemently that he only wanted to return to the King, the owls in their paranoia refused to believe him, or that he was consort of the King. "If you harm a single feather of mine, the King will come and destroy all of you," said the falcon. "Many have been waylaid by outer form: don't let my form beguile you: I am a royal falcon."

Once again, Rumi suggests the truth is found in the inner world, of which this world of sensory forms is but a shadow. The inner world and higher truth is more significant. People in this world of conventional forms and morality often become critical of the seeker lost in divine ecstasy, because they are blind to the higher truth. People usually fear that which they cannot understand.

[Note: these falcon stories on the theme of a rebellious spirit are lifted out of Rumi's original sequence and each is found in separate books.]

> *The King's falcon fled the palace and found his way to the house of an old hag. When she saw the well bred falcon, she cried, "Come, my little pet. Nobody's taken care of you for a long time. Come to mama that she may take good care of you." She promptly tied its feet, clipped its wings and cut its talons. This decrepit, old woman fed it straw.*
>
> *Since even hungry falcons don't eat straw, she prepared a special meat stew. When the falcon showed no interest in her stew, the hag flew into a rage. "Take this, you arrogant, insolent bird," she cried and poured the scalding hot soup on its head. The falcon's crown became bald, and tears poured from its royal eyes. The falcon said within: "The anger of the old crone has blazed forth, yet it hasn't consumed my glory, splendor, self-denial and knowledge".*
>
> *Meanwhile the king searched all day long for his falcon until he came to the hag's hut and spotted the falcon amidst the smoke and dust. The falcon rubbed his wings against the king's hand, as if to say. "I have sinned, forgive me. Have mercy and take me back even though my talons are gone and wings clipped."*

The falcon as the seeker must keep company with the noble and righteous. We cannot place ourselves in anybody's care, but only those whom we can trust. Sometimes even women with the best intentions can cause us much harm. Rumi goes on to give many examples and some more anecdotes of those who lost their way and had to plea for redemption and mercy. He admonishes us that the cause of their straying was often their blind imitation of others.

Rumi alludes to the story of King Solomon, who sent a letter with the hoopoe bird to Bilqis, the Queen of Sheba, asking her to submit to him. Although the hoopoe is not a particularly pretty bird, *"her spirit saw him as the Anqa (eternal life); her senses saw him as a fleck of foam, but her heart saw him as the sea"*. (1603) Rumi frequently compares this world of vanity to the foam in the sea, which floats on the waves and crashes on the shore. In other words, this world is transitory, or temporary, and everything, including us, is swept along by the greater tides. Asleep, we have no control over our destiny, yet we wonder where all the evil comes from.

THE SNAKE

A wise man riding along on his horse one day noticed a snake entering the open mouth of a sleeping man. He hurried over to scare the snake away, but couldn't get there in time. Quickly he began to beat the sleeper with his staff. The sleeper awoke and fled under an apple tree. The wise rider urged the man to eat the many rotten apples which had fallen under the tree. He was stuffing the apples into the man's mouth, as the man choked, sputtered and cried out: "Oh rider, what have I done to harm you? Why do you beat me and force me to eat these apples? Damn, have you lost your mind?"

The rider paid him no mind and kept beating him. "Run!" he shouted to the man, "as fast as you can." As the man ran for his life, the rider came up behind him and beat him some more, so that the man kept falling on his face and was cursing with fatigue. The rider drove him along like this for hours until evening when the man started vomiting. Everything inside him came up, including the big, black, ugly snake.

Still on his knees, totally exhausted, the man gave thanks to his benefactor and begged pardon for all the curses he'd uttered against him. "But you could've told me why you were so cruel."

"No," countered the rider, "you'd have been too terrified to continue the treatment, and so frozen in terror would've died."

Frequently that which we prefer, or like, is harmful to us, while that which we abhor, or dislike is beneficial. Sometimes we're forced to suffer in order to expel the evil within us. This demonstrates the kind of 'tough love' that would be necessary to help a drug addict kick his habit. Similarly we must be merciless with our own nasty habits and weaknesses. In this tale and in the following one Rumi explains how the *enmity of the wise* is preferable and more profitable than the friendship of the fool, wherein lies *woe and perdition*. "To strengthen what is right in a fool is a holy task," states the I-Ching (hex. IV) an ancient Chinese text. Only a holy man can have the patience to tolerate and correct a fool when the opportunity arises. Generally, it's better to avoid fools for their friendship can be dangerous. Looking around this world of vanity, however, we see so much foolishness that it seems unavoidable for us to deal with it. We're obligated to help those who can be saved.

The valiant holy men are a help in the world when the wail of the oppressed reaches them. From every quarter they hear the cry of the oppressed and run in that direction, like the mercy of God. (1934)

RUMI'S BEASTS IN THE MATHNAWI

Although in some traditions, i.e. Chinese, the dragon symbolizes higher, creative power, in this story it represents the lower, sensual self which must be slain. Every call from the lower self, whether lust, gluttony, or avarice, leads to death. Every call from the higher self leads to heaven or bliss. Serve the holy valiant men and so fall under their protection.

"If you're unwilling to serve the holy men, like the bear, you are in the mouth of the dragon. If you cry out, a Master will deliver you and pull you out of danger." (1989) Rumi inserts several related stories within the following one:

THE BEAR

A dragon was devouring a bear when a valiant, young man came to its rescue and pulled the bear from the dragon's claws. With the strength of cunning and courage, he slew the dragon. The bear was so grateful to be delivered from the dragon, he became a servant to his savior. When the valiant man lay down to rest, the bear guarded and watched over him. A traveler passing by was astounded and asked why this bear stood guard. The valiant man recounted his adventure with the dragon.

The traveler said, "Do not set your heart on a bear, O fool! The friendship of a fool is worse than his enmity: it ought to be driven away by every means."

The valiant man considered the traveler's words were spoken in envy. "Look at the affection this bear shows me!"

"The affection of fools is beguiling," said the other. "My envy is better than the bear's affection."

"Go on and mind your business, envious one," replied the valiant man.

22

The traveler tried in vain to convince him to leave the bear, but because of his suspicions he'd hear none of it, so the traveler went on his way. The man fell asleep and the bear sat next to him, driving the flies away. The flies were so persistent that the bear lost patience and became annoyed. He went off and found a large rock to crush them. When he saw the flies on his friend's face, he hurled it at them with all his might. As a result, the sleeper's face was crushed and the flies escaped.

"The love of a fool is for sure the love of a bear: his hate is love and his love is hate. His promise is infirm, corrupt and feeble; his word stout and performance lean... His fleshly soul is in command and his intellect captive." (2130)

In other words, in an enlightened man the governing principle (consciousness) must be awakened and directly linked to the intellectual center. We cannot assume this is true for most people since most of us have forgotten our governor, our Lord, long ago, if indeed we ever recognized him. A Sufi teacher, or spiritual Master, can remind us of this loss, or missing element in our lives. Of all our losses, remembering and restoring this governor would be most important. "Truly those in loss are those who lose their own souls." (Koran XXXIX:6)

Life in this world is full of loss. From birth we lose our connection to the womb to which we continually seek to return; we lose our baby teeth, our innocence, eventually our youth, our hair, our teeth, our health, our loved ones, perhaps even our mind; the list is endless. The more we have, the more we have to lose. Such is the transitory nature of the world; nevertheless, these losses sadden and bewilder us. Simply losing our car keys or cell phones, even temporarily, is perplexing.

We want to be on the path of certainty and to know what's true. Science (the new religion) and other academic disciplines claim to search for the truth. In every field, as in politics, different groups compete to establish their exclusive vision of the truth. As with competing academic theories, so each branch of religion claims it has found the only true way to God. All these competing voices and dogmas are amplified through the mass media so that it becomes bewildering for anyone to distinguish any truth in their arguments.

Along with certainty, everyone seems to want to find true love. True love is very rare, so fortunate is the person who finds it and more fortunate the one who can keep it. Sometimes it's difficult to distinguish between a true friend and a dangerous fool, or between a true spiritual master and a greedy opportunist. Finding a true friend is as rare as finding a hundred dollars on the street, or as is finding a true spiritual Master, one who's slain his ego (nafs) and helps others on the Path without greediness or self- promotion. Often the truth is not so black and white, and a lot of grey area lies in between. Many modern Sufi and/or spiritual groups, for example, are actually cults, yet they manage to transmit a large part of the mystical tradition, and thus can be temporarily helpful. Everyone is searching for their own truth, until they weary of it (accept half truths) and go back to sleep.

THE LOST CAMEL

A certain person lost a (she) camel and asked if anyone had seen it. Once he offered a reward, people came forth with hints and clues as to where the camel was last seen. None of these clues seemed right. Once again, the seeker had to fall back on his own inner certainty, the truth within, that he'd find his camel.

The message is we have to stay alert and trust our intuition. But what happened to the camel? Perhaps something small diverted her. *"Since wisdom is the faithful believer's stray camel, he knows it with certainty..."* (3591) The believer's faith provides him with certainty: faith is more powerful than simple belief.

THE CAMEL AND THE MOUSE

A small mouse caught the leading rope of the camel and gleefully pulled her along. The mouse swelled large with false pride. The camel following behind also followed the mouse's thought. "Enjoy yourself," said the camel inwardly. "Soon I'll show you who's boss."

The traipsed along until they came to a wide river. Suddenly the mouse stopped, paralyzed with fear. The camel said: "Oh companion, why have you stopped? Step forward like a man into that river. You're supposed to be my fearless guide."

The mouse replied: "That's a huge river and I don't wish to drown."

"Oh blind mouse, how could you get all anxious about a bit of water? It barely reaches up to my knee."

"What's small for you is huge to me," replied the mouse. "Your knee is well beyond me."

The camel said: "Next time don't behave so boldly. Stick to your own kind: a mouse has nothing to say to a camel."

"I repent," cried the mouse. "Help me across this dangerous water!"

The camel took pity on him. "Jump up, sit on my hump and I'll carry you across."

Rumi goes on to suggest that a vassal shouldn't pretend to be lord. If you're not spiritually perfect, don't pretend to be a spiritual master. *"Leadership is poison, except to the spirit that from the beginning has in himself an abundance of the antidote."* (3464) The antidote is the selfless dedication and compassion to serve. Many leaders let their pride and arrogance lead them astray. If you find a true spiritual master, you must serve him. *"Don't find fault with the servant of God: do not suspect the King of being a thief."* (3477) It isn't our place to criticize the spiritual masters: we cannot judge them since they operate on a higher level.

THE MIRACLES OF IBRAHIM

Ibrahim, son of Adam, was a king who one day renounced his throne. He had gone out hunting and in hot pursuit of a deer, became separated from his party. His horse was sweaty and weary, yet he galloped onward. Deep in the wilderness, the deer suddenly turned around and spoke to him: "You were not created for this...that you might hunt me. Suppose you catch me, what would be the result?"

Ibrahim was shocked to hear these words of the deer and crying aloud, flung himself from of his horse. He found a shepherd in that lonely desert and convinced him to trade clothes: "Take my royal robes and jewels and horse and give me your rough gown. Tell no one what has happened to me." In that rough gown, he went on his solitary way. He desired to catch the deer, but God caught him through the deer.(Discourses, 170)

Ibrahim journeyed for many months until after a while he sat down by the sea. He was stitching his Sufi cloak when a royal knight walking by spotted him. This knight had been one of the King's servants and recognizing him, immediately bowed down low. He was astonished at the King's transformation into a dervish Sheikh and marveled that he'd given up a grand kingdom for a life of poverty. The Sheikh read his thoughts instantly. The Sheikh took the needle with which he had been working, held it up to the Knight and threw it far into the sea. Then in a loud voice he called for the needle. A multitude of fish appeared on the surface of the waves; each fish carried a golden needle on its lips, saying: "Take, O Sheikh, God's needles." The Sheikh turned to the knight and said: "Is not the kingdom of the heart better than the rotten kingdom I once possessed?"

Rumi goes on to state that such miracles are nothing but a taste, a whiff, of the divine, which is the sweet reward of those who renounce their worldly pursuits. [The story of Ibrahim and the deer is actually found in Rumi's *Discourses* and not the *Mathnawi*.]

Our spirit is more than the spirit of the animals, because it has more knowledge; and the spirit of the angels is more is more than ours, because it transcends common sense. (3327)

Since the spirit of the perfect saints has become superior and passed beyond the limits of man and angels, the soul of all things has become obedient to it. (3333)

The aim of such saints isn't to make an ostentatious show of miracles. Miracles, after all, are simply phenomena which defy common sense and cannot be explained by 'science'. Miracles occur when they are necessary and usually are hidden from most of us. The aim of saints is not to go around performing miracles in order to gain popularity, but to become one with the divine luminous wisdom. A reason exists for every act of creation.

For holy men, having recognized the unity of all creation, reading other people's minds or thoughts is easy. Such a perfect man realizes he is God's minister on this earth and takes responsibility for His creation as was originally intended. Most men have forgotten their

Creator and hence their solemn obligation to preserve and protect this creation. In their 'normal' state of heedless forgetting, polluting the environment or slaughtering all the animals into extinction causes no qualms of conscience. The holy man, however, recognizing the unity of all creation, does his best to protect the poor creatures, and they, in turn assist him whenever possible. Sheikh Ibrahim in the story is such a perfect man so that all the fish in the sea are ready to drop everything to come to his aid.

Obviously most men only dream of having such power over all of creation, but then most men would never willingly renounce all their comforts and riches for a beggar's life out on the dusty road. The greater the renunciation so sweeter is God's reward. In the midst of hunting the deer, King Ibrahim realizes he's wrong to hunt this poor, harmless creature and that animals also have feelings.

Rumi's masterpiece encompasses all living creatures of sea, land and air. He concludes the second book with the story of the ducks, which are at home in all three elements.

THE DUCKS

You are the offspring of a duck. Your mother was a duck of the water; your nurse was of the earth. The desire in your heart for the sea- you get that instinct from your mother. Your desire for land you get from your nurse. Forget that nurse, for she's an evil counselor. Leave the nurse on dry land and come into the sea of spiritual reality. Fear not this sea, even though your mother may warn you of its dangers. Angels do not walk on land, and most animals don't go to sea. Your body is of the animals, and your spirit is of the angels, so that you may walk on the earth and also in the sky. We're all water birds familiar with the language of the sea. Therefore the sea is our Solomon, and we are as birds in Solomon, moving into everlasting life.

Though this last story may seem far-fetched, we need not take these words literally. Rumi frequently speaks in metaphors, and "The Ducks" is all analogy. As Darwin ascertained, all life evolved from the sea before marching onto the shore. Humans are comprised of 90% water. "Don't fear the sea", refers to the sea as the universal reason, the divine influence, where this world with all its money grubbing, pie in the sky schemes, is the foam floating on its surface. As humans and especially as spiritual beings, we need not fear any of the elements, for all is within us, including fire. He doesn't mention fire here since that's a bit more complicated and involves Iblis.

BOOK III

THE ELEPHANT

In India a group of poor travelers, weary and hungry from their long journey came upon a sage sitting by the road. In his wisdom he greeted them warmly with compassion, and they gathered around him.

"I know your bellies are empty and you're ripped with pangs of hunger, but for God's sake," he advised, "don't eat the flesh of a young elephant! You may soon see some on the road ahead and may be tempted to hunt them since they are weak and very fat. But I warn you, their mother is not far behind, and if you hurt her children, she'll come after you for revenge. She'll smell your breath and if you've eaten her baby, she'll kill you. So be content with the herbs and berries you've been eating and don't chase the elephant cubs. I'm trying to save you grief, so listen to my counsel." They nodded, and he bid them farewell.

As they continued walking, their hunger grew. Suddenly they saw a fat, young elephant crossing the road. Like ravenous wolves, they cut it down, roasted and ate its flesh. Only one of their group abstained from eating the baby, because he remembered the words of the sage. He pleaded with the others also to abstain, but in vain.

After their feast, they fell down and slept, except for the hungry one. He saw the terrible mother elephant come running towards them. First, she smelled his breath, but didn't hurt him. On every sleeper she smelled her baby's breath and quickly trampled and tore him apart.

I t has been said that elephants never forget, and indeed true stories of recent times have been told of elephants who hunted down killers of their babies for many miles and days. Clearly, mammals have maternal love for their off spring, too, and mourn their dead.

Rumi often instructs by analogy and this story compares the pious to God's children. Like the elephant, God will wreak vengeance on those who harm the pious saints. They are like wretched orphans alone in this dismal world, despised and exiled. All the prophets were persecuted for speaking the truth. Free from the dominion of their ego (nafs), their worldly greed vanishes. Slander and calumny of the holy ones is compared to killing the baby elephants. In a world full of material pursuits and sensual pleasures, the pure, holy ones are often viewed with contempt and suspicion. Suffering and affliction is their trial. Because their faith is unshakable, their vision extends to the end to when they return to the Creator and those who demonize them will be cast into the fire.

"Grief is better than the empire of this world, so that you may call unto God in secret." (202) and "...how may victory be won without spiritual warfare and patience?" (211)

Indeed, most of the Koran consuls forgiveness and turning away from the Evil ones for "we shall drive the sinners to hell like thirsty cattle driven down to water". (Koran XIX:86) As the founding fathers of America wrote on the back of their money: "Trust in God". Thus, the weak and oppressed need not despair, but have faith the Almighty will resolve their difficulties. Nevertheless, we need allies on this earthly plane who can help us for next to nothing can be accomplished alone.

"Take not unbelievers for friends rather than believers: do you wish to offer God an open proof against yourselves?" (Koran IV:144)

Nevertheless, the question of whom to trust, Rumi cautions, is not always clear cut in this world of duplicity and deception. We seek the true friend, the true Master, but most people wear masks and pretend to be someone else. Often they delude themselves into believing they actually are this false personality. Over time, however, friendship is tested, and the truth is revealed.

THE JACKAL WHO PRETENDED TO BE A PEACOCK

A jackal fell into a dyeing vat for a while and when he came out, his skin was multicolored. "Hmm, seems I have become a peacock," he muttered, glancing at the charming brilliance of his colored fur. Gleefully he pranced before the other jackals in his multicolored coat.

"O little jackal, you joyfully celebrate your difference from us. What has made you so arrogant? Is your ecstasy divine or impudently deceitful?" demanded the other jackals.

He nipped at their ears. "Don't run from me. Behold my glorious beauty and radiant splendor! Bow before this manifestation of divine grace! I've become much more than a mere jackal."

Those jackals circled him with curiosity. "Well then, what shall we call you, radiant creature?"

"I am a brilliant peacock," he replied.

"Do you walk like a peacock as if in a rose garden and do you

have a high cry like a peacock?"

"Uh, no."

"Well then, you are no peacock," they all agreed. "The peacock's feathers, this robe of honor, has been bestowed by heaven. How can you achieve this by pretenses?"

One way to know a person is through his speech. Before he, or she speaks, we have difficulty distinguishing a person's character. Rumi quotes the Koran: "You will surely know them in the perversion of their speech." Another way to see them is through their eyes.

Rumi goes on to compare the peacock to Pharaoh, who also felt he was divine and should be worshipped, because he'd fallen "into a vat of riches and power". 'Pharaoh' is a person who makes an ostentatious display of power and riches, so as to feel above, or better than, others. He tries to lord his riches over others and command them, yet inwardly he's a wretched hypocrite.

Like the *Koran*, the *Mathnawi* gives consolation to the poor and oppressed, for most of the world is indeed poor and oppressed. Prophet Mohammed, peace upon him, said: "My poverty is my glory". As Jesus observed, "it's harder for a camel to pass through the eye of a needle than for a rich man to get to heaven". (Mark 10:25) That's why Jesus told the rich man to renounce his wealth if he wanted to follow him. Clearly, rich folk are too attached to their riches to make progress on the spiritual path. The prophets spoke in parables, or symbolic language, for we learn best by analogy.

Delusion is a multi-faceted jewel. Riches may distort our vision one way, while unloading some of these riches through generosity could also culminate in self-serving delusion if we seek worldly recognition for our acts.

Lest we feel too secure in our virtue, Rumi warns us we all have demons lurking with us, like a hidden dragon waiting to burst forth.

Remember: the greater jihad is against the self, the ego (nafs), which has myriad ways to deceive us.

THE SNAKE CATCHER

A man went into the snowy mountains to catch a big snake. He caught snakes in order to amaze foolish people who come to gawk at such exhibits. Instead of a snake, he found a huge, dead dragon, which filled his heart with fear.

"Wretched man does not know himself: he has come from a high estate and fallen into lowlihood.(1000) Why has he become amazed and fond of a snake?" (1002)

The snake catcher took that huge serpent to Baghdad to stir up excitement and make a little money. "Come look at this dead dragon that I hunted," he shouted. "I suffered much to drag it here." He thought it was dead, but he was mistaken. Although frozen by frost and snow, it was very much alive. The showman set up his exhibit on the bank of the Tigris and a large hubbub arose in the city of Baghdad. Many fools were attracted to see this rare, marvelous beast. The snake catcher waited for a large crowd to assemble in order to milk as much money from them as possible. The idle babblers packed round him in a ring. As he moved the cloth covering the dragon, everyone strained to get a better view. He'd covered it with a lot of cloth and bound it with thick ropes. The hot sun of Iraq, though, had revived the frozen beast, and it began to stir. As the huge serpent uncoiled itself, the people, shocked and amazed, began to yell and shriek. The dragon burst its bonds, and the people fled in terror. The hideous dragon glided forth, roaring loudly like a lion. In the mad hysteria hundreds of people were trampled to death. The

36

snake catcher, paralyzed with fear, cried: "What have I brought from the mountains to the desert?" The dragon devoured that idiot in one mouthful.

For Rumi, the dragon is the sensual soul, which is kept frozen by grief and poverty. *Keep the dragon in the snow of separation from its desires; beware, don't carry it into the sun of Iraq.(1057)* So we must be merciless with our sensual ego, freeze and mortify it, for it deserves no special favors. We must struggle against those lower desires and do what "it" does not like. Once we start to yield to the sensual self, it overpowers and destroys us. We have to distinguish between the world which we perceive through our senses and the spiritual world, which is invisible but nonetheless exists and influences this world of appearances. Once we slay the ego, or sensual self, we're admitted into the spiritual world of love and harmony.

The snake catcher was gobbled up at the end and got what he deserved, for he wanted to promulgate promiscuity or sensuality in order to profit. In his greed he wanted to produce spectacles to enthrall crowds of thrill seekers. He was a showman or lowly pimp, yet this sort of entrepreneur is richly rewarded by our society. Many celebrity announcers and TV hosts could fall into this category and see how rich they become.

THE SHAPE OF THE ELEPHANT

Some Hindus exhibited an elephant in a dark house. People couldn't see in the darkness and tried to tell by touch what was before them. One person's hand fell on the trunk and he said: "This feels like a water-pipe. Another touched the ear and said it seemed like a fan. Another felt the leg and said: "This feels like a pillar." The fourth person felt the broad back of the elephant and compared to a throne.

In this famous Sufi story each person perceived the reality differently, depending upon which part of the animal he touched. Similarly, each person perceives reality differently, according to his/her conditioning and essential nature. For example, a depressed person sees only gloom and doom in the world in contrast to an optimist who sees golden opportunities. Those who seek success in the material world miss seeing the spiritual world, upon which the material world is dependent. The spiritual light is veiled for a reason: like the sun its brightness would blind us. Or Rumi compares the world to a tree and we are like unripe fruits clinging to the bough. When we ripen or mature, we fall away from this world of appearances where nothing is as it seems.

THE MULE'S COMPLAINT
TO THE CAMEL

The mule said to the camel: "In very hill and every valley and difficult trail, you never fall on your face, but go happily along, unlike me who's constantly falling on his face, like someone lost in the sauce. I become beaten and bloodied and fearful to continue. How do you escape such calamities? Tell me the secret of your success so that I may emulate it."

The camel replied: "My eye is clearer than yours and also I have a higher viewpoint, so with my lofty vision I can see further. I can clearly see all the highs and lows ahead and thus avoid falling and stumbling, whereas you can barely see a step or two in front of you."

"All that you say is true," said the mule tearfully and fell at the camel's feet. "Please bless me by taking me into your service."

"Now that you have confessed, you are saved from the evil fires of ignorance. Fear not, for I shall guide you to the Light," the camel assured him.

Thus Rumi asks: *"Are the blind and the seeing equal before you?"* In other words, those with clearer vision who can see beyond this immediate moment, or this sensual world, those who understand the deeper causes and long lasting effects are obviously superior to those who are blind to the hereafter. Such vision, however, requires a certain faith or belief in the higher good, or God.

"For those believe not, there is a deafness in their ears, and it is a blindness in their eyes." (Koran XLI:44)

The mule is like the weak fool who continually breaks his vow of penitence and sins indiscriminately. Through lack of resolve he becomes a laughing-stock in the world. He gets knocked around by indiscriminate blows and the Devil spits on him. Until he finds an intelligent, faithful man to serve and to guide him, he's lost in this world.

The Koran is full of stories of the prophets who were usually rejected by their people and worse. The common people, fixated only on this material world, would demand proof or miracles, so that they could believe the message of the prophets. Although the prophet's message, or warning, was eventually proven true (as in Sodom & Gomorrah), at the time the people were deaf and blind to it because they stubbornly refused to believe without any proof. The naysayers told the following story to demonstrate they had no fear of any prophetic warnings:

THE HARE'S AMBASSADOR TO THE ELEPHANTS

The beasts of chase were sorrowful because a herd of elephants had taken over their watering hole. Deprived of the spring water and in dread of the elephants, they made a plan to send the hare to mediate their concerns. From a nearby hill on the new moon the old hare cried to the elephants: "O king of elephants, I am the ambassador of these beasts and as such immune from your wrath. The moon says: 'O elephants, depart from this spring of mine. If you refuse to leave, I will make you blind and I am not responsible for what will happen to you if you continue to trespass. Depart from this spring so you're safe from my moonbeams. The truth of my warning will be that in the full moon's reflection when the elephants drink, the spring will be disturbed.'" Indeed, it came to pass, that on the full moon when the elephants put their trunks the water, the water was disturbed. The elephants believed the hare's prophecy and departed in fear.

People often say: "I'll believe it when I see it", yet sometimes they refuse to believe even after 'proof' is provided. Therefore, after telling this story, these unbelievers said: "We're not like these silly elephants, terrified by the moon's reflection. The prophets admonished them: "No, you're even more foolish!"

Similarly some folks claim they will reform themselves after a certain time has passed. The following anecdote points to such backsliding:

THE DOG'S VOW

In winter the dog huddles small his body against the frosty winds and swears when it warms up again to build a stone house for protection. But when summer comes, his bones expand in relief. He grows stout and sleek and slinks into a shady spot. "What need have I for a house?" he asks lazily. His belly full, he's content to sleep away the hours, even though his conscience still nags at him to build a house.

So, too, many people fail to take precautions for difficult times ahead. Once our problems have been resolved, and our greed has grown stout, we become heedless and smug and no longer make efforts to improve ourselves. Rumi urges us to give thanks for our blessings and gifts, "*because thanksgiving brings you to the abode of the Beloved*". Be mindful from where all these blessings flow: all comes from Allah, or God, and returns to Allah.

THE EAGLE AND THE PROPHET

When the Prophet Mohammed, peace upon him, heard the call to prayer, he asked for water so he could renew his ablution, or wash himself. After he'd washed his face, hands and feet, he went to put his boots back on. Before he could take his boot, however, an eagle snatched it up and flew away. From high up in the air a black serpent dropped from the boot to the ground. Then the eagle returned the boot to the Prophet. The Prophet thanked the eagle and said: "While I thought you were being rude, you were actually showing me kindness. I felt aggrieved, but you took away my grief. Pre-occupied with myself at that moment rather than with others, I might've died." The eagle replied: "Far be it from me to take credit for seeing that serpent, for I became a reflection of yourself, O Mustafa."

This story is based on a Hadith, or an actual, verifiable event in the life of the Prophet. The lesson, Rumi says, is not to feel sorry for any loss in our lives. We cannot see the higher divine design and may actually be better off without that possession. Sometimes one small loss prevents other greater losses. Life is filled with loss and we shouldn't take any of it too seriously. We must try to stay joyful, even in the face of great loss.

Additionally, the story reminds us that although we strive to be independent and strong, all of creation is interdependent. Sometimes even the smallest, least likely creature can be of assistance. Humans are weak and frail and easily forget, which is why we have to help and support each other, especially in times of need, to remember.

THE LANGUAGE OF
THE BEASTS AND BIRDS

A young man came and asked the Prophet Moses to teach him the language of the animals that thereby he might learn something of spirit and religion.

"Be gone," said Moses. "Abandon this vain desire for it's dangerous to know too much. Seek your lesson and spiritual wakefulness direct from God, not from words and speech."

The man became more eager after Moses refused him, since man usually craves that which he cannot have. He persisted and would not be put off from this desire.

Moses said: "O Lord, the Devil must've twisted this youngster's mind. It will be harmful to him if I teach him, but if I don't he will despair of all religion."

God spoke: "It's okay, Moses, teach him. In our loving kindness we try to answer everyone's prayer."

Moses said: "Surely he's going to regret this desire. Such power is not meant for everyone. The devout are better off staying weak and humble."

Weakness and poverty are security against the tribulation of the covetous and anxious (fleshly) soul of man.

God spoke: "Grant him his need. Let him choose the good or evil."

Choice (free-will) is the salt of devotion. All creation ends up serving God, yet how man does so and to which station he attains must remain his choice: heaven or hell.

Once again Moses admonished the young man: "Abandon your vain desire and fear God."

The man said: "At least teach me the language of the dog and the domestic fowl."

Moses agreed: "You know best! This much will be revealed to you."

At dawn the young man stood at his threshold awaiting him. The maid shook out the table cloth from the last night's meal and a piece of bread fell out; a cock quickly snatched it up.

The dog howled: "You're most unfair, you nasty thief! You have corn and grain to feed on all day, but this crust may be all I could get."

The cock replied: "Be silent and not sorry, for God will give you a bonus tomorrow when the master's horse will die. That'll be a feast day for all dogs."

After the man heard this speech, he quickly sold the horse, and the dog held the cock in contempt. The next day the cock again carried off the bread crust.

The dog snarled: "O beguiling cock, you're an unrighteous liar. Where is that horse you promised would die?"

That knowing cock said: "His horse died somewhere else. He sold it to avoid a loss, but tomorrow his mule will die. That will be great fortune for all dogs."

The covetous man immediately sold the mule to avoid the loss.

On the third day the dog accused the cock: "O Prince of liars, where is the mule?"

The cock replied: "He sold it in haste, but tomorrow his slave will die. Then the next of kin will scatter pieces of bread for all dogs and beggars."

When the master heard this, he sold the slave and was joyful he'd avoided another loss. Meanwhile, the disappointed dog meant: "O driveling cock, perhaps now your days are numbered. How long can you keep telling your lies?"

"I have been most truthful," assured the cock, "as I must since the world depends upon me to awaken them. The master has simply been very clever to avoid loss, but tomorrow he will certainly die. His heir in mourning will slaughter a cow, and you are guaranteed to have a feast."

The wicked man heard of his own death from the cock and grew pale and trembling. He ran to the door of Moses and cried: "Save me from this doom!"

Moses said: "Go and sell yourself and avoid the loss! Since you've become an expert in avoiding loss, escape from death if you can! I knew this would be your fate if you persisted in attaining your desire, but you wouldn't heed my advice."

"O don't rub it in," wailed the man. "I was unworthy to receive this knowledge, but now forgive me for my sin."

"An arrow shot rarely returns to the archer," said Moses. "But I will pray to God that you take the Faith with you when you die, so this lesson will not have been in vain."

The man fell ill with pains in his heart, and they carried him back into his house.

At dawn Moses prayed for the man, that he be forgiven and take the Faith with him. God agreed to bestow the Faith upon him, and even to raise him back to the living if Moses wished. "Nay," answered Moses, "this is the world of the dying, a transient world, and he is better off in the everlasting."

God bestows blessings and gifts and wisdom upon those who are worthy and who can keep silent about these gifts. Such special powers are not for everyone and come with added responsibilities and dangers. People often seek magical powers or short cuts to alleviate their suffering or achieve their goals. Usually their ego dictates their need to feel better or smarter than others. This story teaches us to rest content in the knowledge we have and not to rise above our station. Knowledge is power, yet for us, as weak humans who have difficulty controlling ourselves, too much power can be very dangerous. We're blinded from the truth of God for a reason: it would be too much for us to absorb, as would looking into the sun blind us. The seeker of knowledge in the story was blind to the consequences of receiving it, yet Moses (and God) was merciful to him by assuring him a place on the Path.

Obviously animals have their own languages. For instance, in recent years scientists have learned a great deal about the language of whales and dolphins, and how they communicate across great distances. The story of Moses and the language of the animals shows us that most of Nature's mysteries are veiled from us for a reason. Weak minded individuals can easily abuse this knowledge as witnessed after the atom was discovered in the last century. It didn't take long for the feeble minded humans to develop a mighty, all destroying bomb from the tiny atom.

"But those who were blind in this world will be blind in the Hereafter, and most astray from the Path." (Koran XVII:72)

Instead of seeking super human powers, Rumi encourages us to practice ascetic discipline, to fast and pray, so we can save our soul after we give up our body. Our bodies are borrowed and our world is temporary, yet we are so attached to both that we don't want to sacrifice either. Fixated on our vanity, we shut our eyes and refuse to see the end. This world is a narrow prison full of noisy, heedless fools, and the next world a welcome release from this trial. Thus, we do well to remember our imminent death.

THE GNAT AND THE WIND
BEFORE KING SOLOMON

The gnat came from the garden to demand justice from King Solomon, saying: "O Solomon, you who deal justice to the animals, devils, men and jinn, help us gnats, the weakest and frailest of creatures." So Solomon had to ask: "Against which oppressor are you demanding justice and equity?" The gnat replied: "My complaint is against the power of the wind. His oppression torments us."

Then Solomon said: "O dear gnat, know that before judging every case, God has commanded me to hear both litigants, or both sides of the argument. Go and bring your adversary before me."

"That sounds reasonable and easy enough to do," said the

gnat. "My adversary is the wind and he is in your jurisdiction."

The King shouted: "O Wind, come and defend yourself. The gnat complains of your injustice."

The Wind heard the summons and rushed in rapidly: the gnat immediately took to flight. Solomon said: "O gnat, where are you going? Stop, so I can pass judgement on you both."

The gnat cried, "O King, his very being gives me no rest and causes my death. I cannot help but fly away."

This amusing fable reminds us that even the tiniest of God's creatures is important in the divine design. While gnats are often thought of as pests, they, too, wish to live and thrive. We must respect all life, for we all go to die and return to our source.

Rumi compares the gnat to the seeker of God. When God comes, or when we find God, the seeker, or the self, is annihilated. Union with God consists in dying to the self (fana). Ultimately, everything perishes except for God, the eternal. La ilaha il Allah!

Until that moment of consummation with the Beloved, however, the life long struggle with our selfish desires and lusts (nafs) continues. The following Hadith, or words of Mohammed, peace upon him, explain this necessary battle:

> *"Verily, the most high God created the angels and set reason in them, and He created the beasts and set lust in them, and He created the sons of Adam and set in them reason and lust; and he whose reason prevails over his lust is higher than the angels, and he whose lust prevails over his reason is lower than the beasts."*

Thus, lust and reason, contrary to each other, must come to terms or find a way to co-exist. We cannot deny our animal nature, yet we shouldn't become subservient to it. Rumi identifies a bestial class of men, who are *like cattle*, asleep to the larger world beyond their selfish desires. *"The bestial man is the lowest of the low because he possessed the capacity for transforming himself and striving to escape from lowness, but afterwards lost it.*" (1328) The animals are excused since they know only bestiality. Most of us, since we cannot be pure like angels, have to struggle with our animal nature. The battle of reason against the flesh is like the contention of Majnun with his she-camel.

BOOK IV

MANJUN AND HIS SHE-CAMEL

Majnun was so deeply in love with Layla that he followed and stalked her everywhere, as she kept her distance from this madman. Majnun got on his camel to speed to his beloved, but his camel desired only to run back to her foal, or babies. If Majnun didn't stay alert, the she- camel would change course to return to her foal. Majnun's passion for Layla carried away his reason, but the she-camel was very alert to any slacking in the reins. Perceiving he'd become heedless and dazed, she'd immediately change direction. Under these conditions Majnun was going back and forth for years on a journey which would normally take three days.

He said: "O camel, since we are both lovers and contrary to each other, we are unsuitable fellow travelers. I don't wish to let you go, but with you I'll never reach Layla. It's really not far, but I'm very late. I'm so sick, sick of this riding and full of sorrow and longing." Having said this, he threw himself headlong from the camel onto the hard desert floor. He flung himself so violently from the camel that he broke his leg. He tied up his leg and said: "I will become a ball and go rolling along in the curve of His bat."

The two fellow travelers, Majnun and his camel, symbolize reason and flesh, and are constantly at odds with each other. The spirit must eventually leave the body and its corporeal desires if it is to reach its goal. The spirit wishes to fly up to heaven, while the body has its claws stuck in the earth.

Rumi asks: *"How should love for the Lord be inferior to love for Layla? To become a ball for His sake is more worthy."* With sincerity roll like a ball *"in the curve of the bat of Love."* (1557) (And 'hit it out of the ball park'!) Once we surrender to the divine power of Love, we're pulled along effortlessly and need no longer struggle.

We can surrender our will to divine love, yet we can keep our eyes and ears open and do so consciously and intelligently. We want to be fully aware of the Lord's power and wisdom, so that we may serve the Lord well.

The intelligent man is a guide and leader of men. However, most men are not that intelligent and not cut out to be leaders. Similarly, the rich are few and the poor many; that is not to say that the rich are more intelligent than the poor, although a clever man can more easily acquire wealth. If there were an infinite amount of money, everyone could be rich, but the supply is limited. Similarly wisdom is also a limited commodity, and hence intelligent men are few. Although fools clearly outnumber intelligent men, most people have some intelligence, or are half intelligent. The half intelligent must seek out the intelligent to guide them, otherwise they are lost, bumbling through this world. *If you have not perfect intelligence, make yourself dead under the protection of an intelligent man whose words are living.* (2199)

THE THREE FISH

Some fishermen discovered a lake with some big fish. As the fishermen brought out their nets, the fish noticed and became aware of the danger. The intelligent fish resolved to leave the lake and make the difficult journey onward. He thought: "I won't bother to tell the others for they will weaken my resolve, since I know they love this lake and are deeply attached to it. I'll just go." So he set out from the lake, down the river to the sea. He took the long way and had to jump over many rocks and squeeze through tight spots, but ultimately found safety.

The half intelligent fish was truly sorry he didn't accompany that guide. "I lost that opportunity, but he swam away in such haste. Still, I should've followed him." This he thought, though he knew it's pointless to regret what's past. He was sorry to lose his comrade, but had to think fast how to save himself. To this end, he pretended to be dead and floated belly up on the water. "To die before death is to be safe from torment."

When the fishermen saw him floating, they sighed and said: "Alas, the best one is already dead." The fish, in turn, sighed in relief and thought: "I am saved." The fisherman grabbed him, spat on him and threw him on the ground. The half intelligent fish rolled over a few times and secretly slipped back into the water.

The foolish fish couldn't control his anxiety and kept swimming around in agitation. He leaped back and forth in order to avoid the nets. Inevitably he was caught and placed on the fire. Seething in the flame's heat, reason said to him: "Didn't a warner come to you?" "Yes," he gasped with his last breath. "if I escape, I'll forsake all lakes and live forever in the sea."

Rumi explains that when fools are punished they always promise never to repeat their mistake, yet they almost always break their promise, for they lack faith and are most forgetful. In contrast, wise men learn from their error and take precautions not to repeat it. The first fish symbolizes the intelligent man who can see the end in the beginning. He could be a sheikh and lead the other fish to freedom, but realizing they are too attached to the material world to be helped, he can only save himself. The half intelligent man by becoming aware of the danger can sometimes save himself by pretending to be someone other than he is, or in this case, dead. The foolish one couldn't keep still and thus was roasted for supper. The story also teaches us that when all the world is running around in panic, often we can find a way to liberate ourselves by sitting quietly in meditation. We have to rely on our wits and not be overwhelmed by fear.

This lesson is illustrated by the story of a bird who escaped a trap, which Rumi inserted in the middle of the fish story.

THE LIBERATED BIRD

A man caught a bird in a trap, and the bird said to him: "You've sacrificed many animals and eaten many oxen and sheep, yet none of them have ever satisfied you. You'll get no satisfaction from my paltry body either. Free me, so I can give you three precious bits of advice, and you'll see how wise I am. The first bit of advice I'll give you on your hand, the second on your roof and the third from a tree. Release me and thereby find your good fortune. My first counsel is 'don't believe any absurdity from anyone'." After the bird gave the man this first bit of advice from the palm of his hand, it flew up to the roof of his house. "The second is 'don't grieve over or regret what is past'." Then the bird added: "In my body is a large pearl, almost ten ounces in weight. That unique pearl was the good fortune you missed, for it was not your destiny." The man began to stamp his feet and howl with frustration.

"Didn't I warn you not to regret anything which has passed? Then what are you crying for? Either you didn't understand my

advice or you're deaf. You disregarded my first advice also, not to believe any old absurdity. O noble hunter, if I myself don't even weigh three pounds, how could I carry a ten ounce pearl within me?"

The man wiped his brow and recovered his wits. "Alright, then what about the third piece of advice?"

"Yes, since you've made such good use of my other advice, I should tell you the third piece in vain!"

To counsel a sleepy idiot is to scatter seed on concrete, an exercise in futility. Rumi seeks to sow seeds of divine inspiration, but in fertile ground. Jesus also used this parable of the sower of seeds (Mark 4: 4-10) to illustrate that much wisdom falls on deaf ears. The divine message is of little use to an unreceptive people.

This amusing story runs counter to Rumi's second "Fowler and Bird" story, where the bird couldn't escape the trap. Here this clever bird uses its wits to escape. It also gives beneficial advice: not to be too naïve and not to have regrets.

BOOK V

THE PARABLE OF THE FOUR BIRDS

Abraham said: "My Lord! Show me how you give life to the dead."

He said: "Then don't you believe?"

Abraham said: "Yes! But I need to satisfy my own understanding."

He said: "Take four birds; tame them to turn to you; put a portion of them on every hill and call to them: they will come speedily flying to you.

Then know that God is Exalted in Power and Wise." (Koran II:260)

The Prophet Abraham demanded to see proof of God's power, and, since he was a prophet, God told him to take four birds, cut them up and put each one of their four remains each on a separate hill, the four hills symbolizing the four directions. Then Abraham was to call to each bird in each of the directions, and it would miraculously come to life and fly to him.

Rumi calls for the slaughter of these four evil and foul birds, because they represent the vices of the body within which we are imprisoned.

Cut off the heads of these four live birds and make everlasting the creatures that are not enduring forever. There is the duck, the peacock, the crow and the cock: these are a parable of the four evil dispositions in human souls. The duck is greed; the cock is lust; eminence is like the peacock and the crow is worldly desire. (45)

The crow desires long life or immortality, while the duck is always greedy for more food as if it never had enough to eat. An exposition and entertaining story on gluttony follows, clearly demonstrating these animal vices in humans.

The two faced peacock desires glory and fame in order to catch people. Such vanity is empty and futile, for there is no goal other than *"to catch people with the trap of love"*. Such vain peacocks are caught within the trap of their own desire, *"still busy in pursuit of people"*.

Pursuit of the vulgar is like hunting pig; the fatigue is infinite... that which is worth pursuing is Love alone...Love is saying very softly in my ear: 'To be a prey is better than to be a hunter'. (411)

On this theme Rumi argues as in other poems that it's always better to be a lover than the Beloved, even though most everyone naturally wishes to be beloved. The idea is to love and love some more, without ever thinking of being loved in return, for a return will always come in due time. This world of appearances is really upside down where things are not what they seem: a ruler is really one who serves, while criminals are often hailed as heroes. As stated in the Bible, this world is all vanity, all this piling up of wealth, houses, chattel and children.

Through divine magic fountains become full of fire and stoves full of water. A dish of rice seems like a dish of tiny worms. Among the savages, parents eat their children and children kill their parents. We need not become perplexed or bewildered by this world full of illusions if we remember the Creator, who is all merciful and compassionate.

Among the many miracles the Prophet Jesus Christ performed, he was able to raise the dead (Mark 5:42) (John 11:40), as with Lazarus.

In his humility he claimed he performed these acts as a servant of God. With the grace of God he also breathed life into a clay bird. The Koran, which includes most major biblical prophets, confirms this 'miracle': "God says: 'O Jesus, the son of Mary! Behold, you made out of clay the figure of a bird, by My leave, and you breathed into it and it became a bird'." (Koran V:113)

All religions believe in resurrection or reincarnation of the eternal spirit. The power of the Creator can lift us up again. "Has He not the power to give life to the dead?" (Koran LXXV:40)

The power lies in the breath of life. We take breathing for granted since it's necessary for life and usually flows automatically, but we must learn to breathe, to remember to breathe. This tricky skill is not as easy as it sounds and requires a teacher or guide.

THE ARAB WHO WEPT FOR HIS DOG

A desert Arab sat sobbing next to his dying dog. A beggar passing by asked why he was crying. The Arab said: "Look there at my excellent dog, dying on the road. He was a great hunter and warded off any thieves."

"What's the matter with him? Is he sick or wounded?" asked the beggar.

"He's ravaged by ravenous hunger," lamented the Arab.

"Be patient. Perhaps he's not done in yet," he suggested. After a while he asked: "O noble chief, with what have you stuffed your bag so full?"

"My bag is full of bread and food left over from last night for my journey," replied the Arab.

"Why don't you feed some of this bread and stuff to your dog?"

"My love for him is not that great. Bread and food for travelers on the road costs money, but tears are free. I can shed as many as I want."

"Shame on you, you bag of wind! Since you believe a crust of bread dearer than tears."

In later years they called such useless, hypocritical crying 'crocodile tears'. Rumi says, the greed for eminent power is like a dragon, twenty times greater than the greed of lust, which is like a snake, or the simple greed for food of the duck. The reptilian mind is cold blooded, devoid of the mercy of the heart center. We call such cold blooded tyrants evil, since their domineering ego is ready to sacrifice everyone around them. The ambition to rule is clearly the mark of rebellious Satan.

On another level, the dog represents the carnal nature which must be starved to death. However, sexual feelings are natural for our animal nature, so how far should we go to extinguish them? Through God's grace we receive a multitude of gifts, despite our wicked sinfulness, and giving and receiving pleasure is among these gifts. If we love each other naturally from our hearts without sinful lust, any pleasurable gifts which follow are simply be an added reward for our modesty. "Then which of the favors of your Lord would you deny?" (Koran LV)

THE PEACOCK THAT TORE OUT HIS FEATHERS

A sage walking in the country came upon a peacock tearing out its feathers. "Why, O Peacock, are you remorselessly destroying your fine plumage? You're showing recklessness and ingratitude towards your Creator. Abandon your vain disdain and self-destruction and become content again with your natural beauty."

Evil, self-destructive habits arise from disturbed thoughts and ideas floating in the miasma of a decadent culture which extols savage butchery. Evil eyes of envy may cause us to lose faith in ourselves. Teenage girls become anorexic as they seek to emulate their skinny role models in movies and magazines; boys shoot dangerous drugs because it's cool and to show they have no fear. Thus, the most pure and tranquil soul is disturbed by the violent and perverted images projected on the artificial mind screens (i.e. computers, TV). Images, like the light of God, are food for our soul and not easily erased. Therefore, we should select wisely the images we admit into our consciousness.

Rumi warns us: *"The face of the tranquil soul in the body suffers wounds inflicted by the nails of thought. Know that evil thought is a poisonous nail: in deep reflection it rends the face of the soul."* (558)

THE PEACOCK'S REPLY

When the peacock had finished weeping, he said to the sage: "Go on. You don't understand all the difficulties this beautiful plumage has caused me. These feathers display my pride and free-will, yet I tear them out for they cause my downfall. For the sake of these feathers, fowlers always want to trap me, and archers shoot me. I'm better off ugly and hideous, for at least I'm safe."

According to Rumi, worldly accomplishments and wealth are enemies to the spiritual life. Achieving fame and glory by means of our intellectual talents or physical prowess increases our pride and vanity and exposes us to exploitation. Safety and contentment lies in self-restraint and humility. For example, if a smart man marries a beautiful woman and he would keep her, he would hide her from the world. Exhibiting her beauty for all to see means he will have to share her, and she will no longer be exclusively his. That is partly why many Muslim women cover themselves: their safety lies in modesty. Prophet Mohammed enjoined modesty for women; he never gave any specific instructions, like wearing a chador, or putting a bag over their heads with slits for eyes. Modest Muslim women, who cover themselves, feel free from prying, evil eyes and molestation, for nasty thoughts can be harmful as well as the evil eye.

The noisy, black crows are forever asking for long life. They make their obnoxious cries so they will have more time to sin and eat shit or dead bodies. In any life, long or short, all the moments we are heedless, or choose not to remember God, are a waste of time. For our safety we should avoid such carrion eaters.

THE GAZELLE IN THE DONKEY STABLE

A hunter captured a gazelle and locked it in a stable full of cows and donkeys. The frightened gazelle ran and kicked, futilely trying to flee. The man poured in lots of straw for the animals, and they devoured it hungrily. Since this wasn't proper food for the gazelle, it continued to run about in terror for many days. Tormented, like a fish out of water, it found no peace. The donkeys gossiped with each other: "This wild fellow acts like a prince or king, holding himself so aloof from us." They invited him to dine with them, but the gazelle shook his head, saying: "I, who have eaten the bounty of fine green meadows, could not be content with your hay." "Yes, boast and brag as you fade away from hunger," scoffed the donkeys.

This parable, or analogy, compares God's servant in the world with the gazelle. The food (i.e. pornography and violence) of these godless creatures, addicted to passion and sensuality isn't fit for the holy man. Such blessed servants are rare in the world and seem strange to the worldlings. People fear that which is different and strange, so often the holy man is cast out and persecuted, even by his own family. Everyone desires fine food and music and to be distracted from the cares of this world, yet few see these distractions as snares of the Devil by which we forget God. The following bawdy story shows how easily we can slip and fall from grace:

THE MAID AND THE ASS

A horny maidservant was regularly having wicked sex with an ass. She lay on top of the ass fucking him. As a precaution, the ass had a gourd, or cup, over its penis so it couldn't penetrate her too deeply.

Despite hardly ever leaving the stable, the ass was getting skinnier every day, so his mistress started to wonder, "Why has my ass become so thin?" She asked the smiths and the veterinarians, and no one knew, or could tell. She began to investigate in earnest.

One day peeking through a crack in the door, the old woman gasped as she marveled at the incredible scene. After I examined the matter closely, I saw this narcissistic girl lying on her ass having sex with the ass, she recalled. She became envious and said: "I never thought this was possible, but since it is and the ass is my property, I am within my rights to have it, too. I am willing and eager since the ass has been perfectly trained and instructed."

Pretending not to have seen anything, she knocked at the door of the stable and asked, "O maid, are you almost done sweeping? Won't you open the door, please?" The old woman waited quietly outside, as the maid cleaned up and concealed her secret.

The maid, broom in hand, opened the door with a sour face and tears welling up in her eyes. "Sorry to keep you waiting, mistress, but I had to clean the foul smell from this room."

Under her breath the mistress said: "You sly devil, why has the ass been turned away? Too bad you had to break off from that thrusting, grinding penis to come to the door." But to the maid's face she treated her in all innocence, honorably, saying: "Go take this message for me to our neighbors down the road."

When the old woman had sent her away, she shut the door and filled with drunken, lustful joy, she exclaimed: "I am so thankful for this privacy so I can quench my own lustful fire. It feels wonderful to fool the fool."

Truly, she was the one deluded and was blind to the penalty awaiting her. The donkey lay supine in the same chair she'd seen used by the maid. Vowing to possess that ecstasy, she raised his legs and thrust his penis inside her up to his testicles. The lost lady was 'in over her head' and suffered a stroke. She could not even cry out as her heart shattered. The ass fell on top of her. The stable was full of blood. The woman's head was upside down, her soul carried away to disastrous fate: the scandal of being martyred by an ass.

Meanwhile, the maid on her errand, said to herself: "Ah mistress, too bad you sent away the expert and opened yourself up to danger by foolishly experimenting. All you had to do was ask and I'd gladly have shown you my gourd trick." When the maid returned to the stable, she saw and smelled death and said: "Foolish lady, overwhelmed by the love of an ass, you lacked a skillful guide for your strategy."

This is not the only story in the *Mathnawi* which crosses the line into amusing eroticism, but it's the only one involving animals or bestiality. The highly charged erotic moments in a few of his stories Rumi renders in Latin, presumably not to offend the Muslim clerics of his day. He didn't mind offending the Christian clerics who were well versed in Latin. In the thirteenth century very few people outside of the clergy and government officials were literate. Christianity had already been corrupted, whereas Islam was still new and fairly fresh on the scene. Because journeys in those days were long and arduous, women were often deprived of their men for years when the men went off to fight wars, to make pilgrimages or trade. As a result, women having sex with animals was more frequent than in modern times.

Although he was a pious, ascetic sheikh, Rumi was well acquainted with the lower, animal nature of man, and this humorous story clearly reflects his views. The old mistress has to pay the penalty for succumbing to her lustful desires. The maid escapes since she's knowledgeable and imminent knowledge is power. It's debatable whether many women, who experience sexual urges and lustful desires, burn hotter than men. A man under the power of the bestial soul, or the lustful ego, is more shameful than a horny woman. He has lost the Way and can be tormented by a lifetime of disgrace, whereas a woman should be more easily forgiven. Rumi compares a lustful, shameful man to a menstruating woman, that is, impure or unclean. A balanced life of equanimity, knowledge and contentment satisfies far more than a moment of sensual bliss followed by a lifetime of sorrow and disgrace.

This bawdy tale has several other important instructions. First, it counsels against unsafe, unprotected sex with strangers and/or strange beasts. The main point, however, is that in the fires of lust our perception of reality is distorted and our keen judgment blunted. In the fire of lust, a skanky ass may seem like a youthful beauty, because our "desire makes the heart deaf and blind" (1365). Unless God's mercy, or God's chosen servant, opens our eyes to the dangers of this fiery phantom and guides us back to the Path, we will be lost and disgraced like so many thousands before us.

In modern times the word 'ass' has taken on the connotation of idiot, or an 'aggressively stupid person'. Hundreds of years ago, however, besides being a variety of donkey, which it continues to be, an ass signified lust, wickedness or cruelty, much more than simple ignorance. Many donkeys are actually more intelligent than horses. Of course, the connection between wicked lust and stupidity becomes clearer over time: those who act out their wicked desires are obviously ignorant of their own inherent, goodness and the larger divine design.

Additionally, Rumi counsels that lust arises from immoderate eating and drinking. We must diminish our intake of food, or else marry. "Since you are fond of eating and drinking, ask a woman in marriage..." (1376) Another alternative he hints at is the alchemical process by which the sexual energy can be transmuted, yet he warns of the dangers of attempting this without a proper guide or requisite knowledge.

On yet another level, the maid's story also warns us again of the dangers of blind imitation. The old mistress imitated blindly what she saw without grasping the intricacy of the operation. Rumi mentions the "many impudent fellows who with little practice in the religious life" pass themselves off as spiritual masters. These ignorant imitators, too, have lost the Way.

In the next analogy, or parable, Rumi compares some of the

Sheikh's disciples to parrots, because they foolishly repeat his words in front of people they wish to impress, without understanding their true importance. "He learns the words, but the eternal mystery he cannot know for he is a parrot." (1440) The next parable which follows this theme of blind imitation comes in the form of a dream.

THE PUPPIES WHO BARKED BEFORE THEY WERE BORN

A mystic had a dream he saw a pregnant bitch on the road. Suddenly he heard her puppies howling from within her womb. Startled, he awoke and thought, "Surely, no one has ever heard of puppies barking from within the womb!" He was so perplexed by this dream for many days that he prayed to God for an interpretation. A mysterious voice told him: "This dream symbolizes the 'idle talk of the ignorant' who speak in vain of that which they don't know." A dog's bark in the womb is useless. He cannot ward off robbers since he hasn't seen them. This is like a man wishes to be held in high regard and esteem and babbles nonsense in order to acquire warm admirers. In his vain desire to be held aloft, he misleads others if they accept his prating.

Every earthly desire has its consequences, or price to pay. Everything costs and nothing is for free. If we don't have the material means to pay, we must make big efforts to work hard. Those who are indolent and insolent, who prefer short cuts to hard work, are bound to suffer in the long run. Sometimes payment involves some discomfort or suffering. Then we can be conscious our suffering is a form of payment, or we can suffer blindly, haphazardly, as we're led to our destruction.

The following story adapts that theme and is interrupted by several other stories. Rumi frequently tells several stories simultaneously on the same theme. Several stories will be interwoven within the first, or before the first one is completed. Only those relating to animals are related here.

THE FOX AND THE ASS

The lion was getting old and sickly, but the fox promised to serve him obediently. "I will contrive to bring you a fat ass. Cunning and enchantment is my business. I'll beguile that ass and bring him here," promised the fox.

The fox found a wretchedly skinny ass chewing on some dry thistles and asked the simpleton: "How are you doing in this arid desert of stones?"

"Whether I'm in heaven or hell, this is what God has given me and I'm grateful for it," replied the ass. "I'd be unfaithful to complain. Patience is necessary to overcome every tribulation."

Since we cannot see the end, we "ought not to wish for anything but God's forgiveness and favor". This lesson of humility and contentedness is conveyed by the following story interjected in "The Fox and the Ass":

THE HUNGRY ASS AND
THE ARAB HORSES

A very poor man who sold fire wood owned a hunchbacked ass. This poor ass was in constant pain from the heavy loads it had to carry and the heavy blows it had to endure from its master. It was rarely ever fed and then only dry straw. The royal stable master took pity on the beast and asked the owner why the ass was so bent over. The owner said: "Because I'm so poor, I can barely feed the dumb animal."

"Give him to me for a few days," said the stable master, "so he can recover his health." The owner gladly did so. In the Sultan's stable the ass saw on every side handsome, well fed Arab horses. The stable was swept daily and fresh straw and barley came at the appointed hour. The horses were rubbed down and combed and exercised daily.

The ass lifted his muzzle, crying to heaven: "O Lord, am I not one of your creatures? Granted, I am a wretched ass with back pains and hunger pains so bad sometimes I wish I could die. Why can't I have it half as good as these happy horses? Why must I always suffer such torment?"

Suddenly rumors of war filled the stable. The Arab horses were saddled up and rode into action. Days later when they returned, they were full of wounds on every side. They fell down wearily in the stable and had to be bandaged and cared for round the clock.

The ass heard their moans and said: "O Lord, I'm satisfied with my poverty and hunger. Their food is dainty, but their hideous wounds so dangerous."

Obviously this is a lesson for many of us who suffer and toil through a miserable life. We may wonder at times why has God cursed us with such misfortune, why we can't be happy like our neighbors. "The grass always looks greener on the other side." Instead of complaining like an ass and envying others, we should be grateful for the blessings we do have. Let's return to:

THE FOX AND THE ASS

The fox said: "Lest you become too smug and content, remember we're all obligated to earn our living. Nothing comes from nothing, and we must make efforts to get ahead in this world. ' God gives to those who help themselves'".

The ass replied: "Your faith is weak. 'Trust in God', for God provides for everyone. All the birds and wild animals do not have to go to work and are provided for by nature."

The fox replied: "Your trust in God is exceptional, yet you must recognize your own limitations."

The ass replied: "God's love has no limit for those who deny their own selfish desires."

The fox argued: "God gave you limbs so that you may work and earn your livelihood."

The ass answered: "Trust in God is the best way of earning livelihood, for everyone needs to trust in God and cry, 'O God, bring this work of mine to success!' Nothing is superior to trusting and giving thanks to the Lord for His bounty."

Their argument went on for some time, until the fox duly noted that the ass lived in a barren desert covered with stones. "Move to the meadow down by the river which is like a paradise," suggested the fox. "All the animals live there in comfort and security."

Since he was a stupid ass, he did not reply: "O wretched fox, how come you're so skinny and lean? Why aren't you cavorting in that meadow if it's so pleasant?" Although the ass had spoken of spiritual mysteries to the fox, he had spoken superficially, like an imitator or hypocrite. His greedy desire to eat and drink made him disregard all his previous arguments.

Thus the fox was able to lead the ass away towards the lion in the jungle. At this point Rumi recalls an earlier story where the Sufis in the monastery were joyfully singing: "The ass is gone, the ass is gone." Asses all over the world are always being seduced, but don't you be one, he admonishes. He backs that up that idea with the following amusing story:

THE MAN AFRAID OF BEING MISTAKEN FOR AN ASS

A man ran into a house to take refuge. The master of the house asked: "What's the matter with you? Why are you so pale and trembling?"

"Today they are seizing asses in the streets to do forced labor for the tyrannical king," sputtered the man.

"That may very well be true, but why should that trouble you since you are not an ass."

"They are so urgently relentless in their task, that I may be next," the man answered. "They seem to be hauling off everyone indiscriminately."

B e a man and don't be afraid of those who take the asses," advises Rumi. Then he discourses about the wonders of nature and all the amazing plants and animals. Man is higher than all these, even than the sky and stars.

Even though it's far from Rumi's point and farther removed in history, the story could remind us of how hardly anyone stood up for the Jews when the Nazis hauled them away, and then the Nazis took the gays and the gypsies. Eventually someone had to stand up for humanity, for no one knew who would be taken next.

However, let's return to the fox and the ass:

The fox was leading the ass to the meadow so the lion could demolish him, but when he saw them coming, the old lion was so famished he could not restrain himself. The lion sprang instinctively into attack mode, but was not strong or quick enough to go for the kill. The ass saw him from afar and turned and fled to the bottom of the hill.

"O mighty king, couldn't you have restrained yourself for a few more minutes?" asked the fox. "Then you could've easily vanquished him. 'Haste makes waste': patience and cool calculation is God's grace. Now our design and your weakness is made plain."

The lion replied: "I mistakenly thought I'd fully recovered my strength, but I'm feeble and starving and couldn't help myself. Try to bring him around again with your cunning."

"Yes," said the fox, "perhaps I can make that ass forget his fear and give you a second chance. But this time wait and make sure you have a clear shot."

"Yes," replied the lion. "I didn't realize how sick and shaky I am. I'll pretend to be asleep until he's quite near."

"Assuredly the ass has repented of his error and sworn he won't be duped again," said the fox, "but my cleverness will loosen his vows of repentance."

The fox quickly trotted back up to the ass, and the ass noted: "With friends like you, who needs enemies? What have I ever done to you that you should lure me into the jaws of death? Like the Devil, enemy of our souls, who ceaselessly invites us to our destruction, you don't need any excuse to harm the innocent ones."

The fox replied: "It was a magical spell which made you see a lion. The meadow has such magic in order to protect all the creatures in it. I meant to tell you of this magic, but you were so eager to eat those luscious greens, I thought it could wait. That lion was only an apparition cast by the spell."

"Get out of here!" brayed the ass. "You're an evil enemy indeed! Your ugly, cold hearted face reminds me of the terror I felt not long ago. I have vowed not to listen to your temptations anymore, you ruthless deceiver. What chance would I have in the grip of a lion?"

The fox calmly said: "You fool, you're paranoid and imagining all this. I mean you no harm. Paranoid imaginations have ruined many friendships. Understanding and sincerity is necessary to bridge this gulf of fear and shame. What you saw was simply a fantasy. True friends pardon each other and renounce such delusions."

The ass argued long and admirably (for an ass) against the fox, but his ravenous hunger got the better of him. Any person with half a wit would've simply walked away from the fox. The ass's greed, however, prevailed over his reason. The ass said to himself: "If this really is a plot against me and I die, at least I shall be delivered from this torment of hunger. Perhaps I'm better off dead." He had sworn not to get fooled again by the fox, but his asininity weakened his mind and so he became a willing victim.

The ass followed the little fox back to the meadow and right into the lion's presence. The valiant lion speedily dispatched and tore him to pieces. Afterwards the King of Beasts, thirsty from his efforts, went to the spring to drink some water. Meanwhile, the fox seized the opportunity to eat the ass's choice parts, the liver, lungs and heart. When the lion returned, he wanted to eat the heart, yet could find neither heart nor liver. He asked the fox about these organs which all animals possess, and the fox replied: "If he'd possessed a heart or liver, he wouldn't have come back into your presence a second time".

The fox implied the poor ass had lost his heart and liver from sheer terror. "When there is no light in the heart, it's no heart; when there is no spirit in the body, it's nothing but earth," comments Rumi. (2878) Many hearts are dark, not having received and reflected the light of God. A canal can only be called that when it has water in it; thus, the canals of Mars were long believed to be a myth since they lack water. "A real man has the spirit within him." (2885) Those others appear to be men, but are dead inside, killed by their greed. Thus, a human being, or being human, signifies having a heart and feeling compassion for all living creatures.

"Greed makes one blind and foolish and ignorant; to fools it makes death seem easy," concludes Rumi after this tale. (2824) He claims "hunger is the king of medicines", that fasting opens the door to many mysteries of the spiritual realm. The affliction of hunger is not only healthy for the body, but enables us to have spiritual visions and enter an otherwise hidden dimension.

THE COW ALONE ON
AN ISLAND OF CLOVER

A sweet cow lives alone on a green island where she eats all day from this seemingly endless meadow. She grows fat, but every night she worries: "What shall I eat tomorrow?" So she becomes thin from anxiety, but every morn the field has grown thick again. Again she feeds and grows fat in the day, and worries and gets skinny at night. This cycle repeats itself for years, and she never realizes she has always been provided for, and there is need for her to worry.

T he cow is the carnal soul, and the field is this world, where she (the carnal soul) is made lean by fear for her daily bread." (2865) Once again Rumi suggests we worry too much about acquisitions in this material world. Many people actually worry about starving when the body can go for many days without food.

THE CAT AND THE MEAT

Once there was a man who had a fat, wicked and very voracious wife. Whatever food he brought home from the supermarket, his wife would gobble it up, and he could not object. One day the family guy brought home an expensive cut of meat for a guest. His wife immediately ate it with a glass of wine. When the man came to the kitchen and asked: "Where is that meat? My guest has arrived", she put him off with useless excuses.

"The cat has eaten the meat," she replied. "Why don't you go buy some more ?!"

He went and fetched the scale and weighed the cat. The man said: "You deceptive ogre, that was three pounds of meat, and the cat weighs little more than that. If the cat had eaten the meat, she'd weigh close to seven pounds. So where's the meat, if this is the cat?"

Such small deceptions and lies are typical in the human condition. Rumi asks: If this is the body, where is the spirit? Most people are unaware of their spirit, or have conveniently forgotten it in this mundane world, yet both go together. "The spirit cannot function without the body...Your body is visible while your spirit is hidden from view", yet you need both to function in this world. (3424)

By losing touch with our spirit, we're little better than animals. We may claim we're better because we have greater intelligence than animals, yet this cleverness can get us into deeper trouble as well. Losing touch with our spirit or essential nature, while filling our big brain with all sorts of silly ideas then causes a whole host of psychological problems. Once again our ego (nafs) deceives us into thinking we can weasel our way around these obstacles.

BOOK VI

THE FOWLER AND THE BIRD

A bird flew into a meadow and found a trap set by a fowler. Some grain lay scattered on the ground, and the hunter lay in wait for the ambush. He'd camouflaged himself with leaves and grass and covered his head with roses. The little bird hopped around innocently and approached the man. "Who are you, all covered with grass and leaves?" chirped the bird.

"I'm an ascetic on retreat," answered the man. "I am content to live in harmony with nature and don't need people's friendship. I am aware that death comes to us all too soon, and so God's friendship is more important than people's. I choose to live in seclusion far away from the thieves of the marketplace, who steal our repentance and resolve. We waste half of our lives seeking charming friends and the other half worrying about enemies we've inadvertently made."

Here Rumi makes an astute observation on the human condition. Full of vanity, we worry too much what others think of us. Gurdjieff labeled this fault as 'internal considering', when we consider too much other people's feelings for us. Instead, he suggested we should use 'external considering'; that is, we ought to be thinking how we can improve another person's condition, perhaps in small ways by arranging the pillows to make them more comfortable, by freshening their drink, opening a window, etc. 'External considering', however, requires 'self-observation', or being able to step out of the situation and regard ourselves objectively; that is, we must become fully conscious of our situation.

Most people, however, follow blindly like sheep and haven't achieved that level of consciousness, which requires some effort. Next Rumi interjects the anecdote of man whose ram was stolen:

THE MAN WHOSE RAM WAS STOLEN

A man was leading a ram down the road when a thief cut its halter and took away the ram. As soon as the owner noticed his loss, he ran everywhere looking for his stolen beast. Totally perplexed, he came to a well where the thief was sitting and crying: "Oh alas, alas, poor me".

"What's the matter with you? What are you crying for?" he asked.

"My wallet full of money has fallen into the well. If you go down and get it for me, I'll gladly give you a hundred dollars."

The owner of the ram said to himself, "Why, that would cover the cost of several rams. If one door is shut, another opens. God will compensate me for my loss." He took off his clothes and descended into the well. Then the thief stole his clothes as well as the ram.

Prudence is necessary. Offers too good to be true often are. The Devil is a mischievous shape shifter. Seek refuge with God, who alone knows how this cunning thief steals souls.

The country bumpkin in this story is obviously bumbling through this life obliviously like the majority of us, half asleep. We wonder how long it took him to notice the loss of his beast. Then he was fooled not once, but twice, so we can say 'shame on him'. The ram represents will power and often the world can sap us of this in various ways. Once our will has been diminished, we become vulnerable to other sorts of thievery. So again, the advice is wake up, stay alert and conscious. Back to the bird and fowler:

> *The little bird said: "Solitary retreat is not good for Muslims. The Prophet has forbidden monasticism. Muslims are meant to pray together, patiently bear the afflictions of the world, and benefit God's creatures."*
>
> *"I don't wish to associate with idiots and clods," replied the fowler, "for that's what the world is full of. They're dead in their hearts and corrupt in their souls."*
>
> *The bird answered: "Firmness of heart is needed for achievement, and a firm friend does not lack friends. Be a firm friend that you may have many friends, for without friends you will be left helpless. Without comrades you'll fall into trouble. Don't let the thieves carry off your clothes. Don't travel alone unless you're an ass! The road to God is full of self-sacrifice, yet with companions your progress will increase a hundredfold. True believers are meant to help each other." The ascetic raised contrary arguments, and they debated vehemently on this topic for some time.*
>
> *Finally the bird asked: "Whose grain is lying there?"*
>
> *"It belongs to a lone orphan and was deposited with me since I'm considered trustworthy," replied the man.*
>
> *"I'm really hungry," chirped the bird, "and wish to eat some of this grain, of course with your permission, O trusty master."*
>
> *"You must judge if it's really necessary," replied the man. "If not, you commit a sin. It's better to abstain, or at least promise to pay it back."*
>
> *Although the bird pondered deeply, its hunger pangs pulled it astray from the path of reason. After it had eaten the wheat, it remained in the trap. Weeping and crying was useless after it had succumbed to greed and desire.*

"So this is how those who listen to the beguiling talk of ascetics are punished," lamented the bird.

"No, this is how greedy wretches who devour the property of orphans are punished," answered the fowler.

The poor bird wailed and wept with such touching eloquence, so that the fowler trembled at its grief, but could not release it.

Note the classic oriental, circular structure to the story. In the East when a man wants something from another, he rarely ever asks for it directly. Customarily, a long discussion on an unrelated topic, i.e. reclusiveness vs. solidarity, precedes any such request. This prolonged debate in the story was highly instructive and raised a number of significant points. Interestingly, the ascetic point of view, similar to Rumi's own, won.

In the Mevlevi tradition of Mevlana Jellaludin Rumi, dervishes are required to go on a forty day retreat (chilla) where within a small cell they fast and pray. Through such voluntary suffering they are initiated into the wider brotherhood and greater mysteries.

Companions are worthy if they help us to awaken from our delusions and remind us of our nobility, since ultimately almost all of our misfortunes arise from our heedlessness. Worthy companions make us aware of and protect us from thieves. However, if worthy, righteous companions cannot be found, the solitary life is preferred to time spent associating with fools.

THE CAMEL, THE OX, AND THE RAM

While a camel, an ox and a ram were going along the road, they found a juicy clump of wheat grass before them. The ram said: "If we divide this between us, none of us will get his fill. Whoever has lived the longest, let him eat it. Who among us is oldest? Now I have been around so long, I shared pasture with the ram that was sacrificed for Ishmael."

The ox claimed: "I am most senior because I was coupled with the ox that Adam, forefather of mankind, yoked to plough the earth."

The camel was amazed at these assertions and without a word he lowered his head to pick up the bunch of grass in the air. As he finished chewing, he said: "I don't need to make any claims of seniority, since I am larger than you and have the longest neck and superior intellect."

Within this story Rumi mentions Prophet Mohammed's advice to give special consideration and respect to seniors. When Rumi wrote, however, scarcely 200 hundred years after the Prophet Muhammed, vile and vulgar men already held sway and put their elders forward only on two occasions: "Either in tasting burning hot food, or on a ruinous bridge full of cracks and holes." The vulgar rarely pay homage to the Sheikh "without some mischievous idea" in the back of their head. (2462) Therefore, the spiritually perfect man often must veil his light.

THE MOUSE AND THE FROG

A mouse and frog living on the bank of a river became faithful friends. Every morning they'd meet in a special nook to share stories and secrets. In each other's company their hearts swelled with joy, adhering to the tradition: "A united party is a divine mercy." *Good friends bring guidance and blessings to each other; as Prophet Muhammed said: "My companions are like the stars", which guide us through the night.*

One day the mouse said to the frog: "Dear Froggie, I enjoy your company so much in those moments we have together. I cannot get enough of you. Sometimes I wait on the river bank to speak with you, but usually you're out swimming." *True lovers crave and seek each other ceaselessly. In the heart of the Beloved the lover is all, and in the lover's heart is nothing but the Beloved.* "Dear affectionate friend, by day you are my light and by night my comfort. We meet only once a day for breakfast, and that is no longer sufficient, for I long to see your shining face always. Although I am shabby and ugly, by your grace and generosity please share more your time with me. I am of the earth and you are of the water. Merciful lord, I cannot enter your realm, yet since you are master of both, come to me!"

The two friends debated on how to solve this quandary. They decided to get hitched together by way of a long string, which each friend would tie on each other's foot. "By this device we two persons may come together and mingle as the soul with the body," announced the mouse. "Knot one end of the string on my foot and the other end on yours, so I can pull you to dry land."

The frog went along with this plan, but his heart sank with dismay. He thought: "My scatter brained friend is likely to get me all tangled up in a fine mess." *The frog should've listened to his heart, for the heart never lies. Like when a cloud blots out the sun, the heart can sense when wickedness comes. Accordingly it makes itself heedless, accepts fate and shackles its soul. The fallen spirit laments its loss of freedom, yet cannot shake awake and save the master.*

The mouse in love on the river bank was satisfied to tug on that string, saying gaily, "Now my love will come with one pull of my paw."

Suddenly the raven of separation descended and snatched

up the mouse in its talons. When the mouse became airborne, the frog, too, was dragged up from the depths of the river. The mouse lay helpless in the raven's grasp, while the frog dangled from the string below them, suspended in the breeze. People couldn't understand how the raven had caught a frog since that had never happened before. "This is the just punishment for one who consorts with a wicked rascal," muttered the frog.

The body is like a string tied on the foot of the soul, drawing it down from Heaven to earth...how much bitterness does the soul taste from this pulling!" (2735) According to cosmic laws, spirit must, contrary to its nature, descend, so that it may later rise yet again. This law can be illustrated in the rain water, which falls into the streams, rivers and sea only to rise again into clouds. For every hill there's a valley, and this descent shouldn't dishearten us.

More good advice from this tale is to choose our friends wisely. "Alas, for the sorrow caused by a base friend! Seek good companions." (2950) Or, as the proverb says, "birds of a feather flock together". If we hang around wicked people, wickedness our way will come.

"Reason complains bitterly of the vicious, carnal soul. Certainly congeniality is spiritual in origin" and has little to do with outward form. Form resembles minerals and stones, inorganic matter, and does not know congeniality. In this world of appearances where things are not always what they seem, sinners are often saints and vice versa. In some towns the local drunk might be the highest spiritual person.

So much of the truth must be veiled from the many fools who would abuse it. Thus, we should not be so quick to judge others who may seem perverse, as long as they cause no harm. "Blessed is the eye which is ruled by reason; the eye that discerns the end is cool and wise." (2966)

The following anecdote was inserted, or woven into, the middle of the *Frog and Mouse* story since it's also related to the hadith: "I was a hidden treasure and I loved to be known, so I created heaven and earth." The idea here is that the spirit is dragged down into the physical world, as when a baby is born. The spirit comes from above before it enters human form, or becomes an embryo. Even though they went up in the air with the raven, the frog was dragged down by the mouse, representing the material world. Thus, Rumi suggests we should not be naïve in our relationships. Similarly, if we go through life shining and beaming our spiritual light everywhere, we leave ourselves open or vulnerable to predators, as the following story shows.

THE SEA COW

Like other cows, the sea cow feeds on wild grasses on the sea floor and sea shore. It has a large, stout body with short, stubby legs; only the male cows, or bulls, have tusks. Since it's relatively defenseless against predators, it comes ashore to feed in the dark of night. The sea cow carries a royal pearl from the bottom of the sea, which it places on the beach so it can graze by its radiant light. Traders familiar with this strategy, sneak up and cover the pearl with a dark clay so that the beach suddenly becomes dark. Then these men hide behind a tree to observe. The angry bull runs fiercely up and down the beach seeking to impale its enemy. Frustrated, the cow returns to where it left the pearl. There it sees only the black clay and cannot distinguish the pearl underneath. Disheartened the cow returns to the sea and the traders win the prize pearl.

This anecdote hearkens back to an ancient time when sea cows actually existed. These amphibious mammals survived for millions of years, only becoming extinct over a hundred years ago. Their closest relative, a smaller version of them (approximately 3 meters long), the dugong, continue to live on Australia's north shore, although they are gradually dying out as well. It's easy to imagine other marvelous creatures mentioned in myths who existed thousands of years ago, like dragons, cyclops, hoopoe and phoenix. In that era man lived more closely in touch with, and hence had more respect for, nature. The hunters in the story could have easily killed the sea cows, but needed them to keep supplying pearls.

La perla buena is the spiritual light within humans, which is covered with the foam and dirt of this material world. Spirit was cast down into this material body and as people forgot about it, it remained hidden. A few clever folk, those associated with the occult or hidden realms, like the traders in the story, can use this knowledge of energy to their advantage. Those who have discovered the spiritual pearl, or light within, can recognize it in others who also have. The majority of people, however, are blind to the light within, or have forgotten their hidden treasure and do not wish to be reminded of their loss.

'A man sees what he wants to see', or sometimes what others want him to see. Most people are wandering through this world half asleep and are easily open to suggestion. Usually a hypnotic induction is not necessary to gain influence over them.

THE KING AND THE BEAUTIFUL HORSE

A certain Amir (nobleman) owned a very fine horse, of which there was no equal in the land. One morning he was riding along with the royal cavalcade when the king spotted this horse. Enraptured by its beauty and color, the king's gaze followed the horse. God had bestowed on this high spirited horse exquisite qualities: it was elegant, delicate and subtle, yet fierce and powerful.

"I feel bewitched by this divine creation and attracted by more than its superior qualities," admitted the king. This divine attraction seemed beyond reason, so that he begged for God's mercy to help him understand it. When he returned from his ride, he ordered his officers to fetch the Amir's horse.

The Amir was aghast to lose his beloved horse, but he was weak and helpless against the king's command. He could only turn for protection to the Imadu-l'Mulk, to whom every victim of injustice and distress would run. The Imadu was a devout, unambitious ascetic who was highly revered by everyone, including the king, for his sage judgment and insight. He was like a father to everyone in need and often an intercessor before the king. The Imadu would've preferred to retire to a cave in the mountains, but the king had asked him most humbly many times to stay near the court. So the Amir went to the noble Imadu and pleaded with him that the king not take his horse.

The Amir was so convincing that the Imadu wept, became agitated and ran to the court of the king. He had to wait patiently for the king to finish conducting some royal business, so he prayed as he waited that his intercession might not be in error or in vain. Outwardly he seemed calm and reposed, but inwardly he felt bewildered. In this state of uncertainty he observed the officers leading this special horse before the king. No other colt could match its fleet feet and dazzling figure.

The king, again astounded by its radiance, turned to the Imadu and said, "O wise counselor, isn't this the most splendid, beautiful horse?"

The Imadu replied: "O Sultan, even a demon is made angelic by your fond inclination. Whatever you cast your eye upon fondly becomes most agreeable. While this steed is very handsome and graceful, its large head is a blemish. It's like the head of an ox."

These words stirred seeds of doubt in the king's heart and cheapened the horse in his eyes. Truly, the Imadu had a powerful, invisible influence on the king, yet most people can be easily influenced by the power of suggestion once access is gained. Just this one subtle suggestion of blame from the Imadu chilled the King's heart for the horse. He abandoned his own eye and intelligence in preference to the Imadu's. Of course, the Imadu's words were only a pretext to make the horse seem despicable to the king, and it worked. He ordered the horse to be immediately returned to the Amir

Rumi explains, this world appears sweet, but is actually a rotten carcass. Everything is dying, including ourselves, from the moment of birth. Therefore, although life is indeed beautiful and glorious, we are foolish to get attached to any of it, including our own children, for it's all very temporary.

So why did the holy sage help the Amir retrieve his horse from the king? The Imadu was affected by the Amir's deep love he had for his horse, whereas the king was merely attracted by its shining beauty. Beauty is usually bestowed on a creature or creation as a result of some deep love from someone. Of all the gifts that God bestows, beauty is among the first to fade and disappear.

The Amir was fortunate to find such a holy, influential person to intercede on his behalf. Who could we turn to in such a crisis today? The Imadu, however, had no clear plan of action when he went to the royal court. We would expect certainty from such a sage, but instead he felt totally bewildered about how to proceed. Nevertheless, he remained patient and conscious in the moment, and as events unfolded was able to seize his opportunity to persuade the king indirectly.

Often life may become bewildering and upsetting, and we may be unsure where to turn. Clearly, the lesson, once again, is to stay patient, present in the moment, trusting in God and we will find a way to succeed. As the adage goes: where there's a will, there's a way.

THE CHILD AND THE BOGLE

A mother gave advice to her child: "If a ghost comes to you in the night, or if in a frightful graveyard you behold a dark bogle full of rage, keep a stout heart and rush at it, so that it will turn its face away from you."

"But suppose the devilish bogle's mother has told it the same thing?" asked the child. "He may fall on my neck and destroy me since his mother has also told him to stand firm."

The instructor of the devils as well as mankind is the One God: through Him the enemy prevails. On whichever side that Gracious One may be, for God's sake also be on that side.

A bogle is an archaic term for a hobgoblin, an ugly, mischievous, elfin creature, as in the 'bogy man'. It's interesting that the *Mathnawi* ends with a mythical beast and not a real animal. Rumi is not above bargaining with the Devil. Sometimes a bargain is worthwhile, if one soul can be saved rather than letting the whole lot of them rot. The Devil is only fulfilling God's plan, so that what may seem evil and unjust to us, like the taking of innocent lives, is actually part of the grand divine design. Surely, we must stand firm against evil and ignorance, yet we should also heed the words of Jesus Christ and resist not evil. We can only understand this paradox by transcending this world of duality and remembering to be conscious of the One God.